GOD'S
WORD *in*
3D

KENNY A. AJAYI

SYNCTERFACE™
Syncterface Media
London
www.syncterfacemedia.com

GOD'S WORD IN 3D

ISBN: 978-0-9565043-3-3

Published in the United Kingdom by

SYNCTERFACE™

Syncterface Media
London
www.syncterfacemedia.com
info@syncterfacemedia.com

Cover Concept:
Syncterface Media
in conjunction with Kenny A. Ajayi

Foreword

There are two living entities that guarantee the move of God in any one's life. The first is divine knowledge and understanding, and the second is faith. It is God's will that you experience His stability, salvation, goodness, grace and peace in all things and that you fully partake of His divine nature. You are called to glory and virtue despite the devils assaults; and through divine principles you will walk in the entirety of God's plan.

> 'Grace and peace be multiplied to you in the **knowledge** of God and of Jesus our Lord, as His divine power has given to us all things that pertain to life and godliness, through the **knowledge** of Him who called us by glory and virtue, by which have been given to us exceedingly great and precious **promises**, that through these you may be partakers of the divine nature, having escaped the corruption that is in the world through lust'
>
> *2 Peter 1:2-4*

Kenny Ajayi's book, '**God's Word in 3D**' is a unique and significant exposition on the Bible. You rarely encounter a book that so skilfully articulates the essence of the Word, its' power and practical application to day to day living. He has used several illustrations, parallels, testimonies and scientific facts to signpost the Word and prove its relevance in a complex world.

Our world is changing rapidly and priorities are changing too. People no longer consider the Bible the essential God given 'manual' of life; and those who do often do not understand it or know how to maximise it. 'God's Word in 3D' is a fresh, relevant and divinely inspired voice to a needy, busy, hasty and often greedy generation. It both reminds and enlightens the reader of what the Bible actually is and how to make the most of it.

In his book, Kenny Ajayi demonstrates that God's Word is spirit, full of divine life and created all things. He masterly points to its value as spiritual food for nourishment and God's medicine for health. It is light against forces of darkness and reveals to redeem. God's Word is His wisdom and an unequalled resource centre for all endeavours. Without question, scheduled and spontaneous Bible meditation ultimately propels into good success and prosperity.

Friends; a glorious future awaits you. By great Bible insight you will surge forward. Nothing shall be impossible for you as the LIGHT and LIFE of God permeate your being (John 1:4-5; Mark 9:23). Congratulations, it's a new day and no coincidence that this book has found its way into your hands. Settle down and brace yourself for a spiritual boost. Open your heart to the instruction in 'God's Word in 3D' and register as a candidate for great things.

I strongly recommend this book to the 21st century saint. My view is Kenny Ajayi is a quintessential teacher, a Bible expositor and deep thinker. His thoughts are unusually original, particularly insightful and indicative of a clear 'messenger of the New Covenant'. I am persuaded he is anointed for purpose and the hand of God is upon him.

Dr Albert Odulele
Glory House Churches International

Endorsements

In these days of information explosion, rapid technological evolution and entertainment overload, the Bible can sometimes be seen as archaic and irrelevant. This book challenges that notion with fresh insightful concepts, gripping revelations and entertaining thoughts about the WORD. The Scriptures and passages come alive with new meaning, creative presentations and angles you did not see before! Here is a challenge: take God's Word in 3D with you in your back pack, computer case or Louis Vuitton hangbag and see if it does not change part of your paradigm about the Bible....I dare you!!

Dr Jonathan Oloyede
Convener,
Global Day of Prayer, London
Team Leader,
City Chapel London

It has been a pleasure reading God's Word in 3D. I found the experience interesting and rewarding. I enjoyed reading this book.

William Slusser
Principal Associate,
Word Tech,
Rocky Point, North Carolina USA

Dedication

To whom else can I dedicate God's Word in 3D, but to the God of the Word about whom I write? You gave me:

Life by Your Word

The inspiration of 3D by Your Word

The ability to write by Your Word

The stamina to see this project through by Your Word

I lovingly dedicate this first fruit of many more to come to You, the true Word.

Acknowledgements

My thanks go to:

The Holy Spirit, my Teacher. Thank You for all You taught me personally in the Word of God and through the teachers You brought into my life

To my Bible Teachers:

Thank you for giving to the Lord

Thank you for feeding His flock; Thank you for tending His sheep

Thank you for the long hours of study

Thank you for the sleepless nights of prayer

Thank you for giving to the Lord

In Chronological Order:

My cousin, *Pastor P.R.O Adewoye,* look at what came out of the childhood Sunday night Bible Studies

Brother James (who is now a part of the cloud of many witnesses urging me to go for gold), for laying the foundations of my faith in the God of the Bible

Dr. Tim Ajani, for building on those foundations at a very early age

Rev. Paul Jinadu, for modeling a lifestyle of walking with God

Pastor Emanuel Aladiran, for teaching me the value of character

Rev. Kenneth Hagin (who, though dead physically, by faith still speaks), for introducing me to the ways of the Spirit and inspiring a few chapters of this book

Rev. Kenneth & Gloria Copeland, for teaching me faith

Rev. Charles Capps, your teaching inspired a few chapters of this book

Brother Keith Moore, for helping me to develop a deeper respect for the Word and teaching me to be led by the Spirit

Dr. Albert Odulele (my pastor) for modeling creativity and revelation insight in the teaching ministry and invaluable comments on the manuscript

Rev. Ola-Vincent Odulele, for challenging me to new heights of effective communication and beautifying the art of the pulpiteer... You are a poet, painter, and preacher in the pulpit

No good book is written single-handedly. Although a book may bear the name of one author, the truth is that this individual is, like a tip of an iceberg, only the public face of an entire team of faceless and sometime ignorant contributors. Researchers, reviewers, encouragers, financiers and even critics have often worked tirelessly behind the scenes to achieve the final product. This book is no exception.

I also acknowledge the following contributors to this work:

Morenike, you are the girl of my dreams and my toughest reviewer but your love, support and belief in my abilities is second to none. Thank you for spurring me to greater heights. I would choose you again and again and again! Others invested into the book but you invest daily into the author. Watch out, your profiting is about to become obvious to all!

To my lovely parents, **Dad & Mum Kolapo & Mercy Ajayi** for being the vehicle of my entry to the world, giving me a sound upbringing and praying for me ceaselessly. I am eternally grateful for your parenthood

My 'clone', first ever 'roommate' and twin brother, **Ayodele**, you are a unique blessing from God. Being a twin is a blessing but being a monozygotic twin is a one in a million blessing. Thanks for your editorial acumen; you are a giant in your own right

To my baby brother and researcher **Oluwaseun**, for your sharp review of the manuscript and invaluable suggestions...to my sister **Adebola**, your life is a testimony that this book is not theory but God's Word is indeed medicine. You are such an inspiration. To my sister **Olubusola**, I have seen your life changed progressively in the last few years by the Word in 3D

To my friends:

Foluso Oyerokun, you brought an erudite dimension to the review of this book. I am grateful for your friendship

SAY (Adekunle Oluwanle), I am grateful for your review, research and encouragement

Dr. Jonathan Oloyede, for your support and valuable contributions to the manuscript

Funmi Akinsola ('BS'), you are one of the finest examples of the Christian species and sticklers for the Word that I have met. Thank you for your friendship, prayers and review

Cynthia Eguridu - Thank you for your professional overhaul of the manuscript and above all, your ethos of never being the one to 'throw the first stone'

Kunle Raji - Thank you for valuable comments

Contents

Introduction

*I*n 2003, my wife and I were on holiday in Los Angeles. We took the opportunity to visit the Universal Studios. We even saw a film in the amphitheatre. It was my first ever experience of watching a film in 3D. I will not forget the experience anytime soon.

At the beginning of the film, we all had to put on 3D glasses. The experience seemed normal enough apart from the glasses and the unusual proximity to the characters in the film. Although, Morenike and I were sitting about half way to the back of the theatre, the characters seemed so close that it sometimes felt like we were actually part of the cast and were right in the middle of the set. Everything in the film felt unusually real but we were enjoying the closeness to the action and the intrigue of feeling like part of the production, until the unexpected happened.

Like a bolt out of the blues, the movie switched to a rat infestation scene and commotion broke loose in the auditorium. Screaming, shouting and terror took over the atmosphere. People were jumping out of their seats and climbing on other viewers to get out of the pitch-dark auditorium as quickly as possible. Since we were so close to the action, it felt like these life-like rats were literally inches away from us. It was that real. At the same time, the vents under the seats began to blow with about the same intensity, as you would experience from a rat running over your legs.

The thought of having rats in the room was ridiculous but somehow we accepted it as reality because we were viewing the film through a pair of 3D glasses. Reality had been altered by the perception imposed on us by the glasses. Our actions were governed, not by actual reality, but by our perceived reality. Reality and perception had swapped places. Perception had become reality and reality had become perception. We had somehow made a mental leap from our seats onto the film set, from the audience in a movie theatre to part of the cast and from the security of a modern theatre to a rat-infested city. In the circumstance, the reaction of the audience was perfectly normal. Such is the effect of modern 3D technology and the power of perception!

What could have made fully-grown men and women to lose their decorum to that extent in a public theatre? The movie was so powerful and effective because it was so real. It was so real because it was in 3D. The characters looked like they had the usual dimensions of height and width (seen in ordinary movies) but also a third dimension of depth, which made them life-like. The term 3D (*Three Dimensional*) refers to something which has dimensions of depth, height and width. The expression also describes a consideration of many aspects of a certain subject. This is exactly what the film did. It showed the many dimensions of the characters until they became life-like. An ordinary

2D film would most certainly have failed to provoke the same response from the audience.

3D imagery shares a common quality with the Word of God. God's Word is multidimensional. It has depth, breadth and height. In my study of the 'innumerable aspects' and the 'infinite variety' of the applications of the Word of God, I have made some life changing discoveries, and the book you hold in your hands is a catalogue of these discoveries. The discoveries began at a fateful December prayer meeting.

"Next year will be a year of manifestation of diverse dimensions of my Word"! With divine clarity, unmistakable certainty, and resolute conviction, those words came alive in my heart. 'Manifestation of diverse dimensions of my Word'; what on earth does that mean? Could this refer to a season of practical demonstrations that God's Word is still relevant to everyday life? The presence of hundreds of other believers at this December evening prayer meeting, did not take away from the intensity of the message in any way. The Church was in the middle of a week of fasting and prayer and we met every night for corporate prayers.

I did not fully comprehend the meaning of the message at first. Due to the setting at the time, I assumed that it was only a Word for the local Church. In hindsight, the meetings were perfectly timed for me to receive a personal word from God. For a number of years I have made a habit of spending quality time in prayer sometime between November and December to seek direction for the coming year. These meetings neatly fitted into that scheme.

As the New Year unfolded, I began to see various demonstrations of the Word of God in practice. First, it was in corporate Church life and later in my personal life. Some of these experiences were new to me but others were familiar. Despite this apparent familiarity, I discovered that I had not previously understood or fully comprehended the depth of the familiar manifestations. This was the beginning of an exciting discovery of the multiple attributes of God's Word; its character, practical demonstrations, and applications. Unknown to me, I was entering into an adventure in the riches of the nature and the operations of God's Word in its manifold dimensions. What I learnt has changed my life forever. I share the insights I gained and experiences I had during this amazing period on the pages of this book.

I conclude this chapter with three reasons why you should understand the many aspects of the Word of God. The first is that you can only benefit from a concept to the extent that you are aware of it! Much awareness brings much benefit and poor awareness yields limited benefit. My prayer is that as you read this book, your understanding of the multidimensional nature of the Word of God will open up to you benefits that you never even knew existed.

Liberation from Babylonian exile remained a mirage until Daniel discovered by an understanding of the books, the dimensions (*number of years*) stated in the Word of God (*prophecy*) to Jeremiah regarding the desolation of Jerusalem and the years of Babylonian captivity (*Daniel 9:2*). I believe that as you read this book, you will receive divine insight that will propel you to unthinkable heights of greatness. A momentary revelation of the true nature of Jesus (the Word of God in flesh) transformed two sad, timid and bewildered disciples into jubilant, bold, witnesses of the resurrection, on the way to Emmaus (*Mark 16:12-13; Luke 24:13-35*). Two disciples on the Jerusalem-Emmaus route who were anxious to retire into the safety of their Emmaus home because of dusk, suddenly acquired a boldness to travel all the way back to Jerusalem just because their eyes were opened to a discovery of the true 'form' of the Word of God in flesh. My conviction is that as you encounter the message in this book, timidity will give way to boldness in every area of your life, in Jesus name.

In contrast to Daniel and the Emmaus disciples, Zachariah became muted for a season because he failed to discern the gravity (*dimensions*) of the prophetic word from the angel Gabriel (*Luke 1:18-20*). Yes, this was a prophetic word to an aged childless priest. Yes, it was glad tiding of the impending birth of a long-awaited son, but more than that, this was a prophetic word about the forerunner of the Messiah (*John 1:20-23*). The prophecy had far-reaching dimensions for Israel, for Christianity and the entire human race. The ancestry of the forerunner of the Christ, the earthly ministry of the Messiah, and the salvation of humanity are just a few of the issues of eternal consequence wrapped up in this prophecy. The severity of Zachariah's penalty emphasises the importance of the prophecy.

The second reason why you must understand the dimensions of God's Word is that the term 3D also means '*life-like*'. Therefore, an understanding of the multiple attributes of God's Word will cause the Word to come alive and become real and life-like to you in a manner that you had never dreamed was possible. As we study the Word in 3D, you will see a bigger scope of its character and operations until it becomes life-like to you. Get ready, the Word of God is about to come alive in your situation.

The third reason is that viewing an object in 3D is much more exciting than seeing the same object in one or two dimensions. An insight into the diverse dimensions of God's Word will inject new excitement into your study of the Bible. You are about to wave a permanent farewell to days of boring, lifeless, and abstract Bible study. Your reality is about to change by your perception of the Word of God. You are about to discover an efficacy and power in the Word of God that you have never known, as the Word becomes so real to you. It will become real because you are viewing the many aspects of its operation and character in 3D. You are about to see yourself on the set of a Bible movie.

If you are ready to stimulate your appetite for the Word of God, deepen your understanding of its practical manifestations and increase your capacity to harness its treasures, I encourage you to join me in this life transforming adventure into a manifestation of diverse dimensions of the divine Word in 3D!

Chapter 1

God's Creative Word

⁶³ It is the Spirit who gives life; the flesh profits nothing. The words that I speak to you are spirit, and they are life.

John 6:63

*T*he Word of God is a living entity. This is the first dimension of God's Word that we will consider. *John 6:53-58* is an account of what is probably the most controversial sermon in the teaching ministry of Jesus. This message was so controversial, to the point that by the time Jesus finished, many of His disciples (*not the twelve*) had decided that they had had enough of Him and His ministry. They went back from following Him and never returned (*John 6: 60, 66*). All the same, the teaching in John 6 gives us a profound insight into a dimension of the Word of God as a living entity.

Words - The Smallest Unit of Life

Jesus taught that the Words of God, in His mouth, have

two qualities. They are spirit and they are life. You may say, what does this really mean? In addition, how does it apply to me? Words are not inanimate, they have a quality of life. Just like other living things, words have character; they carry a spirit. Every word you speak is giving life to something. It may be giving life to something good or something bad, but in any event, it gives life to something. You neglect your words at your own peril. You speak flippantly to your own hurt. You throw words around carelessly at your own risk.

How can words be so powerful, you might ask. Scientists have carried out a good amount of research on what living and non-living things are made of. They discovered at a point that all things living and inanimate are made up of matter. The desk at work, the microphone in church and the settee at home are all made of matter. Equally, the human body is made-up of matter. The human body is actually made up of a number of systems. There is a system that controls the water works, another controls the blood and the heart, others control breathing, the functioning of muscles and bones, the production of hormones and the proper processing of food. These systems are controlled by the central nervous system. The systems are made-up of organs. For example, the central nervous system includes the brain, spinal cord and nerves. The organs are themselves made-up of tissues, for example brain tissue. Tissues are similarly made up of cells and cells are made up of matter.

Scientists carried out some work on matter and managed to split it into smaller units. They called these units, protons, neutrons and electrons. For a long time, everyone believed that these were the smallest units of matter. However, on *March 26 2004*, international news magazine Newsweek published an interview with Brian Greene, a professor of physics and a leading academic on the subject of particle physics. This Columbia University academic had recently published information on some ground breaking work that discovered that you could split the protons, neutrons and electrons even further to produce quarks. Quarks further broke down into 'vibrating strings' (*sound*). At this point, you could go no further. In other words, sound making strings were discovered to be the smallest unit of matter. That means the smallest unit of all inanimate and living objects is sound. Guess what? Words are essentially made up of sound. Can you see how fundamental words are to the make up of both living and inanimate things?

Scholars may say that there is no consensus in the scientific community on Greene's theory. I agree. However, this fact does not take away from the point. Elements of Greene's claim are in line with Bible claims, period!

When you call your body healed and your bank account prosperous, although you have symptoms of sickness and your account is in the red; you are essentially addressing the smallest unit of your body and your bank account. You are subjecting your health and finances to a living force, which cannot be resisted. You are addressing the smallest unit of the make up of your body and your finances. Your body and finances therefore, have no choice but to respond. Here is another scripture that states the same truth:

> [1] *In the beginning, God created the heavens and the earth.*
> [2] *The earth was without form, and void; and darkness was on the face of the deep. And the Spirit of God was hovering over the face of the waters.*
> [3] *Then God said, "Let there be light"; and there was light.*
>
> *Genesis 1: 1-3*

Nothing existed before the beginning. The only thing that existed at the beginning was what God said, God's Word. Since words existed before anything else, they are the building block of everything in the world, whether living or non-living. When your world is empty, dark, and void; when everything is without form and chaotic, do not panic; just do what God did when He was confronted by a similar situation and begin to speak. Just like His Words created substance out of void, form out of chaos and light out of darkness, your own words will create what you say in your own world. That is a very bold claim! How can I be so sure of that?

Look at *Genesis 1: 26.*

> *²⁶ Then God said, "Let Us make man in Our image, according to Our likeness; let them have dominion over the fish of the sea, over the birds of the air, and over the cattle, over all the earth and over every creeping thing that creeps on the earth."*

> *Genesis 1: 26*

God made man in His own image. To find out what this means, we must first know what God looks like. After all, how can you expect to know what it means to be created in God's image, if you do not first know what God looks like?

> *²⁴ God is Spirit, and those who worship Him must worship in spirit and truth.*

> *John 4: 24*

The book of John clearly tells us that God is a Spirit. Therefore, man who is made in His likeness is also bound to be a spirit being. There are only three classes of beings that are essentially spirit: God, man and angels. The class of angels includes demons, which are fallen angels (*Revelation 12:7-9*). God is unique in His class. He has certain qualities, which make Him outstanding. Here are a few of them:

Creativity

God is a creative being. In fact, He is the author of creativity. The Hebrew word translated *'God'* in the Genesis 1 account of creation is *'Elohim'*, which means creator. God is the prime creator and the true source of creativity. Every form of creativity can be ultimately traced to God. Obviously, looking at the creativity with which evil is perpetrated in the world, some creative power has been abused. This does not take away from the fact that the creativity originated from God before it was abused.

Creative Words

> *¹ In the beginning was the Word, and the Word was with God, and the Word was God.*
> *² He was in the beginning with God.*
> *³All things were made through Him, and without Him nothing was made that was made.*

John 1: 1-3

God's creativity is accomplished by words. Everything God has ever created was created by words. Nothing that God has ever made was made outside the influence of His Word. God has never yet created anything without using words. This is a very absolute statement. However, it is also a very true statement. It has to be, because the entire universe as we see it was created by words (*Genesis 1, Hebrews 11:3*).

Our understanding of creativity is shaped by what we see in the universe around us. Therefore, if this whole universe, which shapes our understanding, was created by words, then the foundation of creativity has to be words. If God is a creative God and the creativity is in His Words, it means that God's Word is as potent as God is. We can describe His Word as an extension of His being. You simply cannot separate between God and His Word. This is the reason why God is omnipresent (*in all places at all times*). His Word, which is His being, is everywhere, so He is also everywhere all at once.

Umpire of Rules

Another quality that makes God unique in the spirit class is that He is the umpire of the rules that govern heaven and earth (*Genesis 18: 25, Psalms 75:7, 94:2*). God is the custodian of the laws of the universe. He ensures that the laws remain in force to maintain the order of the cosmos. The Bible tells us that He sustains all things by the Word of His power (*Hebrews 1:3*).

This understanding has wide reaching implications. Think about it for a moment, one of the most outstanding distinctions between developed and underdeveloped nations of the world is that the former embrace the rule of law and the latter often do not. I have discovered by observation that a common attribute of underdeveloped nations is a flagrant disrespect for rules. No society will ever realise its full potential until its people learn to respect rules. A society, which fails to commit itself to a set of non-negotiable rules and precepts, is in a constant state of flux; and it is difficult to make progress in such a state of instability.

The rule of law gives us a solid foundation on which to plan and execute our lives. You may moan and gripe about many things that you don't like in the world but you better learn to thank God that He is still in charge of maintaining the integrity of the laws of the cosmos. God may not always influence what a man or woman chooses to sow but without fail, He sees to it that every single time the Law of Sowing and Reaping (*harvest*) takes effect. I would hate to imagine a world where an individual could somehow avoid the consequences of her action by bribing her way to suspending the Law of Sowing and Reaping simply because she happened to have sown some undesirable seeds and was rich enough to bend the rules. We are still answering the question of what it means for man to be created in the image of God.

Creative Man

Do not forget that by the time God spoke in *Genesis 1:26*, all of creation was complete with the exception of man. God had already done the extraordinary. He had brought light, substance and form out of darkness, void and chaos. He had achieved the seemingly impossible. However, with the declaration in *verse 26*, God showed His intention to do something even more outstanding. God was about to exceed Himself, if I may use that term. This time He was not stopping at just exercising His creativity, He was about to create '*somebody*' that would be just like Him; a being that could also create. God was set to make a being that would have the same powers of innovation as Him. This new creature would also have the power to call light out of darkness, substance out of void and order out of chaos.

This being would share a number of God's qualities. This is how Jesus said it:

> [22] *So Jesus answered and said to them, "Have faith in God.*
> [23] *For assuredly, I say to you, whoever says to this mountain, 'Be removed and be cast into the sea,' and does not doubt in his heart, but believes that those things he says will be done, he will have whatever he says.*
> [24] *Therefore I say to you, whatever things you ask when you pray, believe that you receive them, and you will have them.*
> [25] *And whenever you stand praying, if you have anything against*

anyone, forgive him, that your Father in heaven may also forgive you your trespasses.
²⁶ But if you do not forgive, neither will your Father in heaven forgive your trespasses."

Mark 11:22-26

Look at the scripture in *Mark 11:23* and notice the addressee this time. It is addressed to 'whosoever'. 'Whosoever' refers to all children of God because Jesus said in the preceding *verse 22* ' have faith in God' and you can not have faith in God without being a child of God. In addition *verses 25 and 26* clearly show that the subject of Jesus' address are people who have God as their 'Father in heaven'. 'Whosoever' therefore, includes all Christians, black and white, young and old, rich and poor, men and women alike. You can see that Jesus is talking about a law that is universally applicable to all children of God. This means that every Christian is able to say something, believe it and watch it happen. This is a quality that man shares with God: the ability to speak creative words. Just like God, Man is able to use words to create.

Now look at the selection of words that Jesus uses to convey His message. A mountain is a massive geographical structure that is permanently situated in its location. Mountains are not known to move. Therefore, to move a mountain is no mean feat. If that is not enough of a mystery, notice where the mountain would end up once it has been moved by words. Now that is extraordinary. Therefore, Jesus is saying that something as seemingly insignificant as words would uproot something as massive and as permanent as a mountain and then move that mountain a good distance to a sea and then cast the mountain into the sea.

Something else fascinates me about this passage. According

to Jesus, the mountain mover does not even have to push the mountain or exert any physical effort. All he has to do is to speak to the mountain, and the mountain will use its own size, power and might to move itself into the sea. In other words, the same size and might, which made the mountain immovable, in the first place are readily at the disposal of the man or woman who knows how to use words. The speaker does not need a bulldozer. He or she does not need sticks of dynamite; he or she does not even need a workforce, (s)he only needs words and the rest will take care of itself.

Let us paraphrase what Jesus said in *Mark 11:23* like this: A man has the capacity to use his words to demolish any obstacle in his way. He does not need any resources to start with, just words. Any resources that are needed will emerge out of the obstacle itself and avail itself to the mountain mover on his command. That is a display of enormous power!

The Essence of Life

It is no coincidence that God resorted to words when it came time to create the world. Nothing happens in the kingdom of God without words. Words first and other things next! As we saw earlier, words are the very essence of life. Essence is what exists first, and it is the thing that you start with. Essence is what remains when everything else is gone and is broken down. The essence of sweet is sugar. You cannot make sweet without first having sugar. Essence is the raw material from which a product is made. The essence of the human body is dust or sand (*Genesis 2:7*). The human body was created from dust and when the body dies, it returns to dust. The essence of the human being is spirit (*James 2:26*). When the body ceases to exist, the spirit will continue to live on.

If you do not have sugar, you cannot make sweet. In the same way, if you don't speak words you cannot produce anything in the kingdom of God. With that understanding in mind, look at *John 1:1-4*:

> ¹ *In the beginning was the Word, and the Word was with God, and the Word was God.*
>
> ² ___He___ *was in the beginning with God.*
>
> ³ *All things were made through* ___Him___*, and without* ___Him___ *nothing was made that was made.*
>
> ⁴ *In* ___Him___ *was life, and the life was the light of men.*

John 1:1-4

This passage refers to Jesus as the Word of God. The male pronouns '*He*' and '*His*' are used interchangeably to refer to Jesus (*the Word*). Now read that passage again, but this time replace every male pronoun '*He*' and '*His*' with '*the Word*'.

> ¹ *In the beginning was* **_the Word_**, *and* **_the Word_** *was with God, and the Word was God.*
>
> ² **_The Word_** *was in the beginning with God.*
>
> ³ *All things were made through* **_the Word_**, *and without* **_the Word_** *nothing was made that was made.*
>
> ⁴ *In* **_the Word_** *was life, and the life was the light of men.*

Now write out the new phrases and look at the insight we get into *verses 2, 3 and 4*:

- *__The Word__* was in the beginning with God
- All things were made through *__the Word__*
- Without *__the Word__* nothing was made that was made
- In *__the Word__* was life, and the life was the light of men

Let us summarise the four points above. How many things were made through Him (*the Word*)? ALL-things! How many things were made without Him? Nothing! Nothing was made without the Word. All things were made by the Word. The last phrase, *'in the Word was life'*, brings us right back to where we started in *John 6:63*, 'The words that I speak to you are spirit, and they are life'.

Words - An Extension of Life

⁴⁵ A good man out of the good treasure of his heart brings forth good; and an evil man out of the evil treasure of his heart brings forth evil. For out of the abundance of the heart his mouth speaks.

Luke 6: 45

³⁴ Brood of vipers! How can you, being evil, speak good things? For out of the abundance of the heart the mouth speaks.

Matthew 12: 34

Your words are simply an extension of your being. Out of the abundance of a man's heart (*the core of his being*) his mouth speaks. In a manner of speaking, the words that proceed out of your mouth are an extension of the content of the core of your being. So the core of your being is revealed by your words. I am my word and my word is me. My word is simply an extension and an expression of my person. When I speak the Word of God, I am bringing His life and His Spirit to bear on the situation. Whatever Jesus would do if He was present in the room physically, His Word would do when He is present in the room by His Spirit. Therefore, like God's Words are an extension of His being; your words are an extension of your being.

As we saw earlier, the essence of the human being is the spirit or heart (*James 2:26*). Jesus said the words I speak are spirit and they are life. We also saw that there are only three classes of spirit beings in the entire order of creation: God, man and angels (*Psalms 104:4*). Jesus put words in that same spirit class. Since there is no fourth class, we can infer that a word takes on the same nature as anyone of the creatures in these three classes (*God, man or angel*) that happens to speak. Therefore, we can deduce that Jesus means that my Words are exactly the same as me. Since I am spirit and my words are spirit. No wonder, the Bible says in *John 1:1-4* that the Word is God. Here are a few more comparisons between God and His Word. God is Spirit (*John 4:23*) and the Word of God is Spirit. Jesus is the Way, the Truth and the LIFE (*John 14:6*) and the Word of God is Life (*John 6:63*) and Truth (*John 17:17*). You are only as good as your words. If your word is 'no good', then you are no good. If your word is not dependable, then you are not dependable. Your words are as potent as you are.

Finally let's come back to our question, what does it mean for man to be created in God's image? Man is like God in all the qualities we have mentioned so far with the exception that God is the sole umpire of the rules that govern heaven and earth. Man does not share this responsibility with God. On other points that we mentioned, man shares the qualities of divinity.

Let us conclude this chapter by summarising these qualities:

- God is a spirit and so is man
- God is THE creator and man is A creator
- God creates by His Word and man also creates by his words
- Words are an extension of God's being and words are an extension of man's being

CHAPTER SUMMARY

Words are not inanimate, they have character; they carry a spirit and they have life

Words are the smallest unit of all living and non-living things and therefore the building block of life. God uses them to create and so can you

Your words are an extension of your being and the only raw material you need to begin creating your ideal world. Any other necessary resource will emerge from your words and avail itself to you

Chapter 2

Spiritual Food

G od is good with words! Think about this for a minute. God needed to write a manual of life, which would address the multiplicity of human issues, throughout all generations, across all nations and peoples; a document to deal with health issues, relationship issues, money issues, career issues, devotional issues, and political issues, and the list goes on. Somehow, He manages to condense it into a 66-volume book without leaving out any important bits. That is precision par excellence! Only God does that kind of thing. Given the same challenge, anyone else would have written a book large enough to fill the space in the entire universe. God is simply an outstanding communicator.

My pastor takes after his Heavenly Father in the precision with which he speaks. He has an uncanny ability to speak accurately and concisely. On one occasion, I heard him deliver a personal message from the pulpit to an individual in a crowd of hundreds. Everybody in the auditorium heard the words spoken but they made sense to only one individual, the intended recipient. In fact, the vast majority of the audience were unaware of the depth of communication that was taking place. However, the recipient knew that a message was being communicated, that the message was intended for him and that he needed to take action in response to the message. The recipient knew something that nobody else knew.

God is a wordsmith. He always uses precisely the right word for every situation, no more, no less. He always addresses the heart of the issue. God has a way of by passing the side issues to address the heart of a problem. If God ever speaks a word to you, you can rest assured that this is the real issue you need to deal with. God does not waste words. He does not use gap fillers. He is not into small talk or careless chatter. If He ever said something, He said it for a purpose. Listen to this truth spoken through the prophet Isaiah:

> *10 For as the rain comes down, and the snow from heaven, And do not return there, But water the earth, And make it bring forth and bud, That it may give seed to the sower And bread to the eater,*
> *11 So shall My word be that goes forth from My mouth; It shall not return to Me void, But it shall accomplish what I please, And it shall prosper in the thing for which I sent it.*
>
> *Isaiah 55:10–11*

Look at that selection of phrases: *'shall not return void'*; *'shall accomplish what I please'*; *'shall prosper in the thing for which I sent it'*. To return void means to be ineffective. It means to fail in an intended purpose. To accomplish means the very opposite, it means to achieve a goal. That means that every word that God speaks is for an intended purpose and it is sent to prosper in a particular endeavour. You can say it this way, every word that God speaks is selected to convey a specific message and meaning. This is one reason why God uses a lot of symbols and figures of speech in the scriptures. Understanding the way God speaks will change the way you relate to God's Word. Keep that thought in mind as we consider one of the metaphors that God uses to describe the nature of His own Word in scripture. You will see that this symbol shows a certain aspect of the multiple dimensions of the nature of God's Word. Remember that we are still studying the different manifestations of the Word of God in its nature and application.

Word Food

One of the strongest images used to describe the Word of God in the scripture is food. Several passages use the imagery of food to describe the Word: *Luke 4:4; John 4: 34; 1 Peter 2:2; Hebrews 5:13-14* are examples.

> *⁴ But Jesus answered him, saying, It is written, 'Man shall not live by bread alone, but by every Word of God.'*
> *⁵ Then the devil, taking Him up on a high mountain, showed Him all the kingdoms of the world in a moment of time.*
>
> *Luke 4:4-5*

'*Man shall not live by bread alone*'! Is Jesus against the eating of bread? How could He possibly be? He fed the five thousand (*Mark 6: 41-44*) and the four thousand (*Mark 8: 7-9*) with a few fish and a few loaves; He broke bread and ate with His disciples at the celebration of the last supper (*Mark 14:22*), and after His resurrection He invited Peter and the other exhausted disciples to a breakfast of roast fish at the Tiberias seaside (*John 21: 13*). It is obvious that Jesus has no qualms with bread. The message is, to really live, man needs something in addition to bread. Only a certain dimension of man's make up can be satisfied by physical food. Bread is to the human body, what the Word of God is to the human spirit. The bread of the spirit is the Word of God. No wonder, Jesus the Word of God (*John 1:1; 1 John 5:7; Revelation 19:13*) referred to Himself as the Bread of Life (*John 6:35*). So the Word of God is the bread of your real life. Now, somebody may say, okay the Word of God is like bread, right? How do I know how to consume it and how much of it to consume?

Constant Intake

> [4] But Jesus answered him, saying, "It is written, 'Man shall not live by bread alone, but by every Word of God.'"
> [5] Then the devil, taking Him up on a high mountain, showed Him all the kingdoms of the world in a moment of time.

Luke 4:4-5

There are not too many places where the Bible admonishes us to live by something. There are two such instructions that stand out. One is that you must live by your faith (*Habakkuk 2:4, Romans 1:17, Galatians 3:11 Hebrews 10:38*). The other is this scripture in *Luke 4*, where Jesus instructs us not to live by bread alone. Seeing that God is a wordsmith who uses words with purpose and precision, we ought to pay attention to Jesus' careful choice of words.

To '*live by*' means to base ones existence on certain principles. It also means to depend on something for that very existence. Something that you live by is something without which you cannot survive; something that gives you sustenance. So when Jesus says we must live by every Word that comes out of God's mouth, He simply means that when a Christian stops living by the Word, he or she goes into spiritual starvation. The stamina that sustains my spiritual life and yours comes from the Word of God. In the true sense, we really cannot live except by the Word of God. I am not talking about survival; you can do that without the Word. You can survive and get by without the

Word but to really live life to the fullest and benefit from the abundant life that God offers every Christian, you must do it by the Word.

A basic requirement of physical life is that human beings and in fact, all living creatures maintain a constant intake of food. In the same way, the sustenance of the human spirit requires a constant intake of the Word of God. Somebody may ask, *'why do I have to keep taking in the Word of God?'* Well, that would be like a motorist asking why he or she has to keep going to the petrol station to buy fuel. There is only one way to avoid the constant visit to the petrol station: don't drive your car at all. The more you drive that car, the more you have to refill the tank with fuel. Most Christians have no difficulty understanding this principle on physical issues but the same people struggle on the spiritual application.

In the same way that driving a car makes a physical demand on fuel consumption, the process of living makes a spiritual demand on your Word reserve. You do not have to be a preacher, you do not have to be a worship leader, and you do not have to be a missionary; if you are a Christian, the everyday demand of life mandates you to constantly nourish yourself in the Word of God. If you don't, you will become spiritually malnourished.

Recommended Daily Intake

You may agree that you really ought to constantly feed on God's Word but that raises a number of other questions: How much and how often should I read the Word of God? The amount of scripture you feed your spirit depends on a number of factors. At least every Christian should determine to consume a set minimum amount of the

Word of God daily. In other words, you should have a minimum daily intake of scriptures. Every normal person I know eats at least one meal a day, with the exception of seasons of fasting, famine or war. Going an entire day without food, for whatever reason, almost always leads to weakness and tiredness. In fact, nutritionists tell us about a Recommended Daily Intake (RDI) of certain nutrients that the body needs. The RDI for each nutrient varies among individuals depending on age, sex and other factors. I believe that just as the physical RDI varies between individuals, the spiritual RDI also varies.

> *¹ And I, brethren, could not speak to you as to spiritual people but as to carnal, as to babes in Christ.*
> *² I fed you with milk and not with solid food; for until now you were not able to receive it, and even now you are still not able;*

> *1 Corinthians 3:1-2*

Paul explains clearly to the Corinthian Christians why he fed them on spiritual milk. The spiritual diet he fed the Corinthians was simply based on their spiritual maturity or spiritual age. He fed them on milk because they could not digest solid food. Babies can only handle milk. If you attempt to feed a baby on fish and chips, you may kill him because his digestive system is not developed enough to handle solid food.

Paul says the same thing in different words in the book of Hebrews

> *¹² For though by this time you ought to be teachers, you need someone to teach you again the first principles of the oracles of God; and you have come to need milk and not solid food.*
> *¹³ For everyone who partakes only of milk is unskilled in the word of righteousness, for he is a babe.*
> *¹⁴ But solid food belongs to those who are of full age, that is, those*

who by reason of use have their senses exercised to discern both good and evil.

Hebrews 5: 12-14

I suggest from these scriptures that your minimum daily Word intake will depend on your spiritual age, your level of spiritual responsibility, your vocation or life's calling, your particular season of life and the size of your desire for spiritual growth. You would expect the RDI for a Bible teacher to be higher than the RDI for a carpenter or a full time mum. It makes perfect sense that the daily Word intake of a new believer would be less than that of a person who has been born again for decades.

I maintain a daily minimum intake of the Bible. I have a target in chapters of how much I must read daily. I also spend a set time meditating on selected scriptures and I have a series of hand picked personal confessions, which I aim to make often. On top of these, occasionally I would set apart a number of extra discretionary hours on a Saturday to study particular subjects. I have not yet mentioned the additional hours that I spend preparing for the various aspect of my teaching ministry in the local Church.

Let me take a side trip for the benefit of those involved in any kind of teaching or preaching of the Bible. I have noticed a strong connection between the consistency of my personal Bible study discipline and the effectiveness of my teaching. I simply teach better when my personal Bible study is more consistent. The reason is simple. Most of what I teach comes from what God shows me in my personal study. Every one of us, ministers and laity alike, would also do well to set ourselves a target of how much of God's Word we wish to consume daily.

Careful Intake

¹⁸ Therefore take heed how you hear. For whoever has, to him more will be given; and whoever does not have, even what he seems to have will be taken from him.

Luke 8:18

How you hear is as important as what you hear! Apart from a constant intake of God's Word, you also have to make a careful intake. It is one thing to consume the Word constantly; it is another thing entirely to consume the right quality of Word. In other words, constant intake answers the question about how much, that is, the question of quantity. But careful intake answers the question of quality. Some may say how does that apply to me? Well, take the example of an elite athlete. She is very particular about her diet. She does not eat just anything. She carefully regulates her calorie intake and is precise about the proportion of different nutrients contained in her diet. During competition, the eating regime is even stricter. Athletes have simply learnt to regulate their food intake according to the demands of their lifestyle.

It is my conviction that you also ought to regulate your Word intake by the demands on your life at any point in time. Some of us fail in certain seasons of life because we fail to discern the spiritual demands on us at these times. Some are in the middle of intense ministry, some are busy climbing the career ladder and others are just stretching their faith to attain a particular target or goal. Whichever one of these applies to you, the fact is that all these activities demand time and spiritual stamina. All of these seasons simply call for an increase in your intake of the Word of God. It took three years of isolation in the Arabian Desert for Paul to receive the revelation necessary to prepare him for the ministry (*Galatians 1:11-18*).

Sadly, most of us do the opposite of what is required. The busier we get, the less time we spend in the Word. That is like an athlete who for whatever reason is training so hard but is eating so little. When I was a teenager, my friend Kunle, competed in Judo at national level. He discovered on the eve of a certain competition that he weighed several pounds above the weight limit for his category. He only had three options. One was to do nothing and end up throwing away the many months of hard work, discipline and gruelling training by being disqualified. Another was to climb to the next weight category and compete against bigger, stronger and better-prepared boys. These opponents would have spent the last several months preparing to fight in the higher weight category. The last option was to try and lose the excess weight and compete in his preferred category. Eating very little food for a whole day prior to the fight, engaging in strenuous exercise and going to bed in several layers of clothing, to encourage extra weight loss through sweating, were all part of the third option, which Kunle took.

It produced the desired result but at a steep price. Kunle woke up on competition morning and was within the weight limit at the weighing-in ceremony. The only problem was that, the demands of the harsh slimming regime, particularly the intake of very little food, had weakened my friend to the point that he hardly constituted a threat to his opponent. By the time he stepped onto the mat, he was hungry, exhausted and dehydrated. He lost the bout without much of a fight. He had lost the bout before even stepping on to the mat.

You have lost some battles in life; not because of the superiority of the opposition; not because of the intensity of the fight but because you entered into battle undernourished in the Word and lacking in the spiritual stamina needed to defeat an opponent that would have otherwise been a walk over.

Martin Luther[1] , the great sixteenth century reformist, was quoted as saying: *"tomorrow I plan to work, work, from early until late. In fact I have so much to do that I shall spend the first three hours in prayer."* This veteran had learnt a secret of productivity which 21st Century Christians will do well to imitate.

Eating Disorders

A person who continues to under nourish his or her physical body will eventually suffer from symptoms of malnourishment. There is a spiritual parallel to this truth. I know from personal experience that spiritual malnourishment does not always manifest immediately but if left unchecked will eventually show its symptoms. Let us now consider a few common eating disorders and their spiritual parallels.

Spiritual Anorexia

Anorexia is an eating disorder which causes a person to eat less food than her body requires. The hallmark of anorexia is a distorted body image. The condition leads to severe weight loss and an inability to maintain the minimum healthy weight for ones weight and age. Anorexia is caused by a constant deficit in nourishment where the person's energy expenditure exceeds the calorie intake.

The anorexic is simply not taking in enough food quantity. If left untreated anorexia can eventually cause the death of the sufferer. One of the problems is that the anorexic is sometimes unaware of the situation. She therefore wrongly thinks she is eating enough. Only the people around her see the problem. At the same time that observers can see that the anorexic is getting thinner and leaner, the sufferer continues to have a wrong mental perception that she is in fact overweight.

Some Christians are spiritually anorexic. They are not taking in enough Word. Although their spiritual energy expenditure far exceeds their Word calorie intake, the spiritual anorexic fails to rightly diagnose the problem. As physical anorexia is capable of causing death, a spiritual anorexic is in danger of spiritual starvation. The spiritual anorexic may even think she is doing well because she wrongly perceives that she is consuming too much of the Word. Often observers can see evidence of wasting or emaciation. Spiritual anorexia shows its symptoms in lean bank accounts, wasted bodies, thinning (*dysfunctional, nonexistent or unhealthy*) relationships and diminished income flow.

Spiritual Kwashiorkor

Kwashiorkor is another eating disorder that is caused by a person not eating enough protein in his or her diet. Unlike in anorexia, a person suffering from kwashiorkor may actually be eating enough food but in the wrong proportion. So kwashiorkor is a deficiency in food quality not necessarily in quantity. Sufferers show symptoms of tiredness, lethargy and poor immunity to diseases. Kwashiorkor also causes the sufferer's body to grow disproportionately. They develop a large belly and thin limbs.

It is possible for a Christian to suffer from spiritual kwashiorkor. They may be taking in enough quantity of the Word but in the wrong proportion or of the wrong quality. As physical kwashiorkor is capable of causing lethargy, tiredness and poor immunity to disease, spiritual kwashiorkor causes a Christian to be weak and unable to take on spiritually demanding activities. The Christian suffering from spiritual Kwashiorkor may also be recognised by their disproportionate growth. They may be very strong on the doctrine of healing for example but also struggle to pay their bills or live uprightly.

Summary

So, one dimension of the Word is that it is food to the born again spirit. Let me conclude this chapter with a testimony. I recently saw a close example of the positive effect of the constant and careful intake of God's Word. I watched the Word of God over a number of months totally transform a person who was diagnosed with cancer. Even her own doctor did not expect her to live. Unlike most Christians in such situations, this person gave herself completely to the Word of God on healing. She listened to healing tapes, read books on healing, confessed the Word of God on healing over her life and listened to other people testify about healing for several hours a day.

Seven days a week, for several weeks, her main occupation was consuming the Word of God. She jealously and judiciously kept away from anyone who would contaminate her with any contrary thoughts and maintained a constant and careful flow of the Word of God. I watched this dear woman battle through major surgery, a battery of seemingly endless blood tests and scans, hospital admission after hospital admission; and negative news after negative news from doctors. To God be the glory! She is back at home fully recovered and she has returned to work. The constant consumption of the Word of God came through for her. It had to happen that way. The Word of God is an indomitable force! It can never be conquered. No wonder Jeremiah testifies:

> [29] *Is not My Word like fire,' declares the Lord, and like a hammer that breaks a rock into pieces?*
>
> *Jeremiah 23:29*

CHAPTER SUMMARY

God uses words with great care and every word He speaks is intended for a purpose

Like bread nourishes the body, the Word of God is food for the human Spirit therefore no Christian can live to their potential without the Word of God

The process of just living life uses up the Word of God stored in your heart, therefore you should set a daily Bible study/meditation target

Chapter 3

Word Medicine

²⁰ My son, give attention to my words; Incline your ear to my sayings.
²¹ Do not let them depart from your eyes; Keep them in the midst of your heart;
²² For they are life to those who find them, and health to all their flesh.

Proverbs 4:20-22

*T*he Word of God is '*health*' to your flesh. In fact, the word translated health in *verse 22* also means medicine or remedy. This chapter focuses on the medicinal nature of the Word of God. This is yet another dimension of God's Word. The difference between the wise and the foolish is that when serious symptoms of sickness show up, the wise consult a doctor but the foolish self medicate presumptuously! In the natural, a wise person would take the following steps in sequence, when symptoms of sickness show up:

1st   - Consult a doctor

2nd   - Follow the doctor's prescription

3rd   - Stick with the prescription until symptoms leave

4th   - Return to the doctor if symptoms return

Although *Proverbs 4* talks about the medicinal power of the Word of God over physical sickness, this remedy is equally applicable to symptoms of lack, defeat, career regression, relationship problems with God and others and any other affliction known to man. God's Word is medicine to the human spirit. Let us look at how the four steps pertain to the Word of God.

Consult a Doctor

This is the most important step in dealing with symptoms of life's problems. You must begin by getting the doctor's perspective and his diagnosis. The worst thing an individual can do in response to ill health is to wrongly self-medicate. Let us imagine that several individuals develop a headache and all of them foolishly swallow two tablets of Paracetamol (*pain medication*). But on thorough medical examination it turns out that the first patient was really just suffering from exhaustion which presented as a headache.

The second person's headache was due to dehydration and the third individual was suffering the effects of caffeine overdose, having had too many cups of coffee. Our fourth patient had spent the night in a poorly ventilated room and the fifth sufferer had simply had insufficient sleep for a few nights. The sixth person had caught a flu infection and her headache was an early sign of the illness. Inhalation of poisonous smoke was responsible for the seventh individual's headache and the eight person's headache was due to a more ominous medical condition which demanded urgent attention.

Of all eight patients, only one might require a painkiller. A good rest, proper ventilation, plenty of drinking water, and a proper night sleep would be suitable for others in the group. A few of the group would require more urgent and serious medical intervention ranging from poison antidote to chemotherapy or radiotherapy.

Supposing all our patients decided to put themselves on a course of pain medication treatment by default; in the end, only one of them would experience any recovery. Others would risk consequences ranging from periods of discomfort, to serious long term damage to health and possible death. On the other hand, if each of the patients had seen a doctor and got a diagnosis and an appropriate prescription, each would have had a good chance of full recovery.

Friend, take some counsel from the prophet Jeremiah, at the first signs of symptoms of affliction on your character, your health, your finances, your marriage, your children or your job, save yourself the trouble and book an appointment with the Great Physician. This is how the prophet put it: *Is there no balm in Gilead, Is there no physician there? Why then is there no recovery for the health of the daughter of my people? (Jeremiah 8:22).*

There are too many Christians busy swallowing Paracetamol when the real problem is stress, poor ventilation, gas inhalation or dehydration. At best, these dear folks are just masking their symptoms. Learn to get before God and obtain a diagnosis and a prescription for your particular situation. Pray until you get a Word from God. Don't come out of your closet until you have direction on the financial problem. Shut yourself up in your room and switch off your mobile phone, blackberry and laptop, until you hear from heaven regarding that character flaw.

Pain killers do not work on bacterial infections, only antibiotics can cure those and even then certain infections are only sensitive to selected antibiotics. You must find out the right prescription for your condition. Not just any scripture will do. Therefore, do not take a short cut. Avoid the mistake of looking over your shoulders and adopting your friend's prescription by default. Your symptoms may be similar but the conditions are different. Your friend's prescription for her financial woes may be in *Proverbs 13:23* because of a wasteful lifestyle but yours may be in *Proverbs 6:6* due to your laziness.

You have both shown symptoms of lack but your diagnosis are poles apart and your medications completely opposite. You need to work hard to make money but she needs to be smart with the money she makes. She is making enough but you are not. Your problem is in your income but hers is in expenditure. If you hear your friend confessing that she has the wisdom to manage her income wisely according to God's prescription in *Proverbs 13* and you say, '*me too*'. You will keep confessing and watch your situation change progressively. Yes, it will get worse! Get your own diagnosis and prescription directly from the Physician.

Follow the Doctor's Prescription

Once you have consulted God and you have a customised prescription from His Word, the worst thing you can do is to ignore the prescription. Too many people have died by doing just that. Don't use the Word prescription in any old slap dash manner; follow the instruction to the letter. Your deliverance is in that Word; pay attention to the way to you handle it. It is your customized remedy guaranteed to produce results in that situation. Don't deviate from that Word. Your ears have heard the word, saying this is the way, walk in it (*Isaiah 30: 21*) it is no time to gamble and be double minded.

Remember what I said earlier that God does not waste words. Stick with the programme even if it seems ineffective at first. One of the tragedies of Christianity is that too many 'patients' see the doctor, obtain a diagnosis and a prescription and then put away the prescription in the chest of drawers and never use it. Sadly, the medication is not designed to work in the medicine cabinet. It must be swallowed to have any effect. Only those who practise the Word of God will prosper from it. Anything short of that is self deceit. The Apostle James spells it out just as clear as it gets: *But he who looks into the perfect law of liberty and continues in it, and is not a forgetful hearer but a doer of the work, this one will be blessed in what he does.* (*James 1:25*).

Prescribed Dosage

I do not know of any medicine that is not prescribed with a dosage. Have you ever heard a doctor say, *here is an antibiotic; use it as often as you remember*!? No. Doctors are always very precise in their instructions: '*take one tablet three times a day before meals and don't take more than four tablets in any 24 hours. The tablet is not to be taken within 30 minutes of drinking milk.*' Some other medication is to be taken in the middle of the meal and yet others after the meal.

Let me share a personal story to illustrate the point. A number of months ago, I became concerned about some symptoms I was experiencing. I consulted the Great Physician and His prescription was '*cut out such and such from your diet'*. It seemed too good to be true. Alas! After only a few weeks of following the instruction, the symptoms totally disappeared. Occasionally, I have disobediently gone back to the food item in question and the symptoms had return temporarily on these occasions. Here is the lesson: The food item is perfectly legitimate. In fact it is a staple part of most people's diet. However, having consulted the Great Physician, who created me and knows what is good for me more than anyone else, my prescription was to cut down on the intake of this food. To continue to take the same amount of the food item as before would simply be foolish. What is God's personal prescription to you? Follow it!

Regularity of Medication

Let me emphasis a point I made earlier. There are not many medicines that are taken less than once a day. Similarly, God's prescription needs to be taken with regularity and at least daily. God told Joshua to meditate in the Word day and night (*Joshua 1:8*). David meditated in the law of God all day (*Psalm 119:97*).

It is better to ingest a small portion of the Word daily than to take large irregular portions randomly. Medicines work by a build up of certain chemicals in the blood stream. These chemicals are anti disease and when the concentration of the chemicals in the blood reaches a certain level, it completely alienates the disease. One of the best steps you will ever take is to put yourself on a daily dosage of the Word of God once you have God's remedy for your ailment. Then, consciously and purposely build up a concentration of the Word in your system until the point of saturation, at which the Word will displace every symptom of lack, sickness and affliction.

According to Bible teacher, Gloria Copeland, the difference between the doctor's prescription and God's prescription is that the latter has no side effects but the former does. You can overdose on the doctor's prescription but not on the Word of God. People around you may think you are overdosing on the Word but don't worry you are not. In due course, the disappearance of your symptoms will prove you right.

Stick with the Prescription Until Symptoms Leave

The next thing you must do is to stay with the prescription until all the symptoms are gone or the Great Physician changes His prescription.

Return to the Doctor if Symptoms Return

If you consulted the Great Physician at the first sign of symptoms and followed the prescription to the letter, you will recover from your symptoms. Your bank balance will become healthy, your wayward teenage child will return home and you will win your court case. However, the disappearance of symptoms does not mean that you will never have to deal with future problems. If new symptoms ever show up, never resort to the last prescription by default. Your attitude must never be '*the last time I had a financial challenge, God gave me a Word in Philippians 4:19, therefore I am just going to return to the same scripture this time around*'. No, every new attack is symptomatic of a condition.

Jesus has authorized you to bind any opposition here on earth with the promise that heaven will respond accordingly. The promise in *Matthew 16:19* is based on you having the keys of the kingdom. You need the keys of the kingdom to bind poverty, sickness and demonic oppression before you can be guaranteed of heaven's backing. Now notice, that the word 'key' is in the plural form, 'keys' not 'key'. If you have a dozen keys in your bunch and one door to unlock but you do not know which one of the keys is appropriate, you may spend an awful long time in trial and error. Jesus speaks of keys of death and hell in *Revelation 1:18* and again, key is in the plural form. The point is that you need to know the precise prescription or the precise key for every new problem. It is not enough to resort to the last prescription by default.

Joshua was a case in point. On the borders of Jericho, he arguably confronted the stiffest opposition of his military career to date. God gave him a strategy to take Jericho: *walk round the city walls, completely mute, once every day for six days. Do seven laps on day seven and raise a rapturous shout at the end of the last lap (Joshua 6:2-5).* As you well know, the strategy worked and the resistance from Jericho and its walls became history. However, when it came to Ai, a much smaller and less formidable opponent, Joshua stumbled. Ai was so small; the entirety of its name was spelt in two letters! Joshua and all of Israel were presumptuous: *'if we could whip Jericho with its imposing walls and formidable army, what is Ai to us? Let's just send a handful of men. A detachment of three thousand soldiers will do the job.' (Joshua 7:2-5).* You know the story. Failure to seek divine guidance cost Joshua dearly and he lost thirty six men in the only defeat of an illustrious military career that saw thirty one victories in just seven years (*Joshua 12:7, 23*).

Let me take a quick but necessary detour. I have learnt both from scriptures and experience that one of the most vulnerable seasons of life is the period just after a major victory. Such victories may get you thinking you are invincible and that is alright, providing you acknowledge that your invincibility is in God. Otherwise complacency sets in with its wife, vulnerability and their offspring, defeat is usual around the corner. Sadly, you can lose smaller battles than those you have previously won in life if you don't have the right strategy. What was Ai in comparison to Jericho? No battle is too small for you to seek a divine strategy.

Joshua soon realized his error and went back to God. (*Joshua 7:6*). The defeat had nothing to do with the size of Ai. There was sin in the camp of Israel and defeat was certain until the sin was dealt with. (*Joshua 7:12*). Sin is a terrible thing; it makes you unable to stand before your enemy. Sin has a way of making you to lose confidence, forcing you to retreat before the enemy. God showed Joshua how to deal with the sin issue (*Joshua 7:13-26*) and gave him a new military strategy for operation AA2 (*Alienate Ai 2*): Take the entire army, ambush Ai, get a small number of soldiers to lure the men out of the city and pretend to flee before them. Then let the ambush invade the city and burn it down to ashes (*Joshua 8: 2-24*).

We see the same principle of getting a prescription for every situation in the life of Jesus. There were a number of death attempts on His life during His earthly ministry. God gave Jesus a different prescription for each of those dangers. On one occasion, the crowd was ready to assassinate Him by throwing Him down the brow of the hill on which the city was built, but He walked through the midst of them and got on His way, leaving them apparently unaware of His escape. It sounds like God completely mesmerised this angry mob (*Luke 4:29-30*).

On a second occasion, He just stayed where He was but

nobody could touch Him. The mob must have been so much in awe of Him that nobody dared lift a finger. Perhaps God covered Him with such awe that nobody had the guts to attack (*John 7:34-44*). On a third occasion, Jesus hid Himself as the crowd wanted to stone Him, then He slipped through their midst and escaped (*John 8:59*).

My point is that, God's prescription and remedy for Jesus to escape each assassination attempt was different on all three occasions. Why did Jesus have to hide and then escape in *John 8* when all He needed to do in *John 7* was stay still? If Jesus (*God in flesh*) needed a precise strategy for each situation, how much more you and I. I would not like to imagine the outcome if Jesus had decided to simply resort to the default option and stayed put in *John 8*.

In conclusion, I repeat the four steps to applying the Word of God like medicine below:

1st   - Consult a doctor

2nd   - Follow the doctor's prescription

3rd   - Stick with the prescription until symptoms leave

4th   - Return to the doctor if symptoms return

Congratulations, your days of symptoms are coming to an end!

CHAPTER SUMMARY

There is a specific solution to every life problem, therefore learn to pray until God shows you the diagnosis and the prescription (medicine) for the problem in His Word

You must use God's prescription in His Word to see results and do not stop taking your medicine until the symptoms leave

Apparently identical problems of life may have different roots and different solutions in God's Word, therefore ask God for a new diagnosis and prescription of His Word if symptoms of life's problem return

Chapter 4

Light for Life

¹⁰⁵ *Your word is a lamp to my feet and a light to my path.*

Psalm 119:105

*Y*our dad has not arrived yet; something happened on his flight from Saudi Arabia, so his arrival has been delayed. He will be home tomorrow. You can ring him then. Those words concluded my long distance telephone call to my home. I was curious about the on board event that led to the delay but concluded that twenty four hours was not an unbearable waiting time.

I will come back to that story in due course. In the meantime, let us focus on another dimension of the Word of God. This time we shift our attention to the nature of the Word of God as light. You know by now that God and His Word are inseparable. Throughout the pages of scripture the unbreakable bond between Jehovah and His utterances cannot be mistaken. John tells us in his first epistle that God Himself is an embodiment of light. He is light personified and there is no darkness in Him (*1 John*

1:5). Not surprisingly, the Psalmist refers to God's Word as a lamp for his feet and a light onto his path (*Psalm 119:105*). In other words, both God and His Word embody light.

The gospel of John also gives us an insight into this union between Jesus and His word. Jesus, the Word of God who became flesh (*John 1:14*) is also the Light of the world (*John 1:9*). So we see that the Word of God is also the Light of God. This relationship between the Word and Light of God shows up time and again throughout scriptures. In *Acts 9: 3-4*, we read the account of the conversion of Saul to Paul. Saul was travelling to Damascus on a search and destroy mission to Christians. On the outskirts of the city, something unexpected happened. This violent persecutor of saints saw a bright light and the next thing he knew was that he was sprawling on the ground. Then he heard the voice of Jesus. He saw the light of God first and then he heard the voice of God.

Peter had a similar experience in the Jerusalem jail, where he had been detained awaiting execution. His situation was beyond hopeless. He was fastened by two chains and kept between two soldiers. In the unlikely event that he somehow broke the chains and eluded the soldiers, there were two other sets of guard posts and an iron gate to overcome before reaching freedom. On the eve of his execution, an angel of God breached prison security and 'broke' into Peter's cell. At that moment, the light of God shined in the prison and then Peter heard the Word of God from the mouth of the angel (*Acts 12:3-12*). Again the Light and the Word came together.

The Light of the Word speaks of revelation. Now how does this revelation of the Word pan out in 3D? What does light do? Let's consider an answer to this question in the following sections of this chapter.

Light of Life

¹² Then Jesus spoke to them again, saying, "I am the light of the world. He who follows Me shall not walk in darkness, but have the light of life."

John 8:12

Light is essential for life. No wonder Jesus, the Light of the World is also the Light of Life (*John 8:12; 9: 5*). Scientists tell us about photosynthesis, the process by which plants manufacture sugar and oxygen. More than that, there is scientific evidence that growth is limited or nonexistent in plants, in the absence of light. In the unlikely event that a seed manages to germinate in the dark, it almost certainly ends up nonviable and would not survive to reach the usual life span.

We are told that through a chemical reaction powered by sunlight, plants convert carbon dioxide to sugar and oxygen. Both products of photosynthesis are the basis of plant and animal life and are therefore essential for the sustenance of life. In fact, most organisms would die without the continuous supply of these products. In other words, in a certain sense light is the basis of life. Without light there would be no photosynthesis and without photosynthesis there would be no production of sugar and oxygen. Can you see that light is more important than you might think? The physical life of the world's ecosystem will simply not continue without it.

Similarly, your spiritual life is so dependent on the revelation or light of the Word of God. You and I will simply not make it as Christians without the light of the Word. Your present quality of Christian life is a function of the light you have in the Word of God. In fact, this principle does not only apply to believers, it holds true for non-Christians too. This is the reason why the devil keeps the unbeliever from seeing the *'light'* of the gospel of Christ (*2 Corinthians* 4:3-4). The gospel is simply the good news and that good news is the Word of God. Satan knows that if he can somehow blind people from seeing the light of the Word, he can keep them from the life in the light.

Light and Direction

Light provides direction and guidance. I became acquainted with the revelatory power of light a number of years ago. Out of desperation to know my destiny in God and my life's call, I spent an entire month in prayer and fasting, all the while expecting some outstanding revelation from heaven. Really, a vision would have been perfect but failing that I would have settled for a voice from heaven, an angelic visitation or something equally spectacular! But what did I get? I got an impression in my heart directing me to read an entire book of the Bible.

It was not exciting at the time, but many years later, I am thankful that God chose to guide me by giving me revelation in His Word. In hindsight, no vision or angelic visitation would have conveyed the depth, breadth and precision of revelation about my destiny, which I got from that portion of scripture. Today, that book of the bible has become my favourite. When I read the chapters, I get a sense of God speaking to me personally. It feels like God had me personally in mind when those Words were originally written. I see myself and destiny in those chapters so much so that putting my name as the original recipient of the letter would seem perfect to me. Such is the power of the light that comes from the Word.

When light comes, you see things that you otherwise would not see. The Psalmist shares his own experience of the Word. His testimony is that the Word of God is lamp for the feet and light for the path (*Psalm 119:105*). A lamp implies a limited amount of light that provides illumination for a few steps. In other words, the lamp of the Word provides immediate guidance for short term decisions but the Psalmist also says the Word of God is light. Light is symbolic of more strategic direction for long term decision making. The Word of God provides a lamp for your feet and a light for your path. You select a path first before taking steps on that path. So the Word of God is a guide not just for your everyday decision but also for those one in a lifetime choices which shape the course of life: who to marry, what career to follow, to make a vocation of Christian ministry or remain in secular employment.

Light and Protection

Another function of light is that it provides protection. Let me return to the story I started at the beginning of the chapter. My long distance call home was during a corporate time of prayer and fasting, a number of years ago. My father was flying on a transcontinental flight from Saudi Arabia to Nigeria on the second to the last day of the fast. It occurred to me to pray for journey mercies and I did.

I was awoken at dawn by a very strange experience which seemed like a vision. I heard the voice of what seemed like an angel quoting *Genesis 19:21* to me … "*See I have favoured you concerning this thing also, in that I will not overthrow this city for which you have spoken.*" I knew intuitively that this concerned dad's trip and God was giving me an answer to my prayer for his protection. It was settled in my heart that there might be hitches on the journey but dad was protected.

A few days later, when I made a second telephone call home, I discovered that on the very day I had the vision, there were problems on the flight. Midway through, the flight crew announced that the flight had to make an unscheduled landing. The landing was successful but some passengers later reported seeing flames on part of the plane whilst still airborne. Subsequently, the airline admitted that the plane had been faulty. My dad arrived home safely after a 24 hour delay. I am absolutely convinced that the story would have been sadly different had I not got light through the Word of God.

One of the weapons that God has given us against the enemy is the light of His Word. The enemy likes to operate in the darkness of ignorance because his works are evil. God protects you and me by shinning the light of His Word over the activities of the devil, so that we are not caught off-guard by ignorance.

The Holy Spirit speaking through Paul said, we are not unaware of the devices of the devil, lest he should take advantage of us (2 Corinthians 2:11). That means a lack of awareness, a lack of illumination or a state of being in the dark regarding the enemy's operation on any issue gives the enemy an undue advantage. That advantage is neutralised by the light of God's Word. The Word of God makes us aware of Satan's mode of operation. For example we know that he is an impostor (2 Corinthians 11: 14) falsely parading himself as an angel of light. Jesus said it this way: evil and darkness go hand in hand, just as truth and light are associates. The truth of the Word exposes the works of evil (John 3:19-20) and protects you from harm.

Some of the most devastating harm that Christians suffer source directly from subscribing to lies of the devil. There are Christians who are sick today because they believe the demonic lie that God does not always heal His people. Others are languishing in poverty, because they believe that material prosperity is excluded from the salvation package. These dear souls maintain their erroneous beliefs even in the light of a contrary scripture like *3 John 1:2 'Beloved, I pray that you may prosper in all things and be in health, just as your soul prospers.'* The correction and reproof that the Word brings is the only antidote to these situations. No wonder *Proverbs 6:23* says: For the commandment is a lamp, and the law a light; reproofs of instruction are the way of life.

Intimacy and Light

³ Oh, send out Your light and Your truth! Let them lead me; Let them bring me to Your holy hill and to Your tabernacle.

Psalm 43:3

Holiness is a function of one's relationship with God. Holy men and women revere Him so much that they would not venture to do things that upset Him. Therefore Holy persons consecrate themselves to Him and away from all contaminants.

Notice how the Psalmist describes intimacy with God as a by-product of light from His Word. Your relationship with God is only as intimate as your revelation of Him from His Word. No one can relate with another individual beyond their knowledge of that individual. When a woman knows God as a good God, that knowledge draws her nearer to Him. When she is convinced that He is faithful and cannot lie, she is encouraged to take His Word at face value and trust Him against the odds. This is the reason why there are Christians who will not tolerate symptoms of sickness in their body but at the same time have associated with abject poverty all their lives. They have simply become intimate with God as Jehovah the healer (*Exodus 15:26*) by a revelation of His Word but have somehow missed the revelation of Jehovah the provider (*Genesis 22:8*) and are therefore not intimate with Him on that level.

Light and Persecution

It would be a travesty to conclude this chapter without warning you about the persecution, which accompanies the light of revelation. If you study Church history, you would discover that God's revelation of His Word and His person has been progressive. Only a number of centuries ago, being a Christian was synonymous with being Roman Catholic. Then further revelation led to the birth of the Lutheran Church and then the Baptist Church. From the Baptist Church, the evangelical movement emerged and now we have the Charismatic, Pentecostal movement. It is thought provoking that all of these Church movements, without exception, were founded on a revelation of a certain aspect of scripture, which was hidden to the previous movement. However, each of these movements was also persecuted by the previous movement.

So, as you seek God for a deeper revelation of His Word, be excited about the new levels of intimacy with Him and the blessings of short term and long-term direction, protection and a new quality of life; but be equally prepared for the accompanying persecution. This is how Jesus said it to Peter in *Mark 10:30*: those of you who have left family and possessions for my sake and My Word will get back a hundred fold of blessings including persecutions.

Lines in Pleasant Places

I conclude by sharing a testimony of the effect of the

revelatory power of God's Word. A number of years ago, I found myself captivated by a scripture in *Psalm 16:6: 'The lines have fallen to me in pleasant places; Yes, I have a good inheritance'*. I would blurt these words out of my mouth before even getting a chance to think about it. This happened over a period of weeks.

Not long after, it became apparent that the Light of God's Word had been working behind the scenes. Out of the blues, my wife received a phone call about a certain amount of money running into thousands of pounds. This money was her entitlement but she was ignorant of it. Well, to cut a long story short, without any application or soliciting, the money was remitted to her. You might say that was just a fluke. Lo and behold, shortly afterwards a second instalment of money, of which she was similarly ignorant, was sent to my wife from the same source. The lines had indeed fallen to us in pleasant places! You could be the next person sharing your testimony if you would get hold of the light of the Word of God.

CHAPTER SUMMARY

The Word of God and the light of God go together

The light of God's Word brings life, protection, direction
and intimacy with God

The light of God's Word also attracts persecution

Chapter 5

The Power of Revealed Truth

³² And you shall know the truth, and the truth shall make you free.

John 8:32

nother dimension of the operation of the Word of God is the element of revealed truth. The Greek word for inspired truth is '*Rhema*'. Jesus told His disciples, if you know the truth, the truth that you know will make you free. In other words if you see a man in bondage, there is a relevant truth about his situation that he does not know. If there is a woman showing signs of oppression, there is an aspect of revelation about her situation that she is unaware of. I can guess what you are thinking: If all that it takes to be free is to come to the knowledge of the truth, how come there are so many Christians who go to listen to the preacher on Sunday and are still bound by sickness, poverty and defeat? Surely, the preacher preaches the truth. How come his audience is still bound?

That is a good question to ask. The answer is in the meaning of the word '*know*'. To know the truth is to come to an understanding of the truth. It means to perceive and acquire knowledge beyond the surface. To know means to have in depth knowledge, revelation knowledge, and personal knowledge. The word also carries a sense of becoming intimate with something or somebody. In fact, the ultimate expression of the word is in the sense of sexual intimacy between a man and his wife. To know also means to have intercourse with.

Now, this sheds new light on what Jesus said. You will understand the truth and the truth that you understand will make you free. You will perceive the truth and that perception will free you from bondage. You will become intimate with the truth and that intimacy will produce deliverance from oppression. You will have Intercourse with the truth and that interaction will result in emancipation. Rev. Ola-Vincent once paraphrased *John 8:32* this way: *you will know the truth and the truth will manufacture your freedom.*

The first reason why there are people in Church who listen to the Word of God and are no different is that, listening to the preacher is one thing and coming to an intimate knowledge of the truth is another. There is a difference between listening to the preacher talking about his own personal knowledge of the truth and you arriving at your own personal revelation of the same truth. It is one thing to know about healing and hear testimonies of healing and the Word on healing. It is another thing entirely to force feed yourself with the Word on healing until you have a personal revelation, which drives all symptoms of sickness away from you.

Hearing the preacher is only the first step. The word you heard must go beyond hearing. You must be like the noble Berean Christians, who '**_received_** *the word with all readiness* *of mind, and **searched the scriptures daily**, whether those things were so. Therefore many of them **believed**'. (Acts 17:11-12, emphasis added)*.

Notice what the Bereans did. They received the Word, and then searched it daily. They had a quest to see for themselves that those things were true. *Acts 17:12* tells us the outcome of their diligence: *'Therefore, many of them believed'*. Their diligence paid the dividends of personal conviction in the Word and nobility. There are too many unbelieving Christians in the pews because too few take the time to search the scriptures for themselves daily. The truth that manufactures freedom is the truth that you know personally. Much to the disappointment of some contemporary Christians, the pastor's revelation does not manufacture your freedom. Only your own personal revelation can do that.

Am I discounting anointed teaching and preaching? No. We need anointed teachers and preachers. I do some teaching myself. Listen to Apostle Paul's summary of the role of the preacher in *Romans 10:14-15 (paraphrased)*: How can anyone call on God except he first believes that He exists; but how can you believe He exists except you heard about Him; how can you hear about Him except a preacher tells you and how can the preacher tell you except she has been sent and anointed by God to preach? The role of the preacher and teacher is to preach the Word as she is sent and anointed but your role is to do what it takes to believe that Word and make it a personal revelation. That is the kind of Word that leads to personal intimate knowledge and belief in the Word which produces freedom.

Degrees of Knowledge

There is a superficial knowledge of truth and a personal, revelation knowledge of it. If I came into a room full of people and asked, how many of you know David Cameron, the British Prime Minister? Perhaps every hand in the room would go up. *'Put down your hand if you have not personally met the prime minister'*. Except I was in a room full of the political elite, only a few hands would remain up at this stage. *'Put down your hands if you have never been to the living room at Number 10 Downing Street'* (*the official residence of the prime minister*). There would be even fewer hands raised at this stage.

'Keep your hands raised if you have been to the prime minister's bedroom'. It is unlikely that any hands would be up at this stage. But in the unlikely event that there is somebody that intimate with the seat of power, let me ask you to *'only keep your hands up if you have heard the prime minister snore'*. All hands should be down at this stage except you are the first lady, one of her children or close family. Notice that at the outset, everyone claimed they knew the prime minister, but as the level of intimacy came under scrutiny, it became apparent that most people had a varying degree of knowledge and only a handful of people could actually claim very intimate knowledge. The kind of knowledge of the truth that produces victory is the very intimate type, which sadly, only a few have cared to acquire.

Too often, the reason why many listen to the Word and few receive from it is that there is a failure to understand, or perceive the Word to the necessary degree. There is a lack of intimate exchange with the Word; therefore the Word does not manufacture freedom.

Mind your Business

Whose business is it to know the truth? Yours! Whose business is it for that truth to produce freedom? That's the business of the truth. Too many Christians are trying to mind God's business for Him whilst they leave their own business unattended. My business is to interact with the truth until I know it. God's business is to see to it that the truth that I know actually delivers on the promise on the packet. Trying to mind God's business means, asking questions like, *how can I be sure that this Word will deliver if I give myself to it? I know about so and so down the road who confessed the Word until he went down the tube. What if my confession produces the same result?* That is not your business friend. Mind your own business and give yourself to becoming intimate with the truth. God is good at minding His own business. His Words never return to Him void because He is not a man, that He would lie (*Numbers 23:19; Isaiah 55: 11*).

Have you ever heard of a man standing by the pool and saying, "*my only concern is that I may get into this pool and not get wet? All I just want is to be wet, but I am afraid to jump in, in case I don't get wet. Are you sure I will get wet if I just jump in?*" What would you tell such an individual? '*You just jump in first, then you will find out. The moment you jump in, you are no more in control of the situation. The water does what it was designed to do*'. Similarly, the Word of God is designed to produce freedom. If the Word ever gets access into your spirit, the rest is history. The only possible outcome is freedom.

Word Seed

Do you remember the parable that Jesus spoke in *Matthew 13:4-8, 18-23* about the Word of God and its resemblance to a seed?

> [4] *And as he sowed, some seed fell by the wayside; and the birds came and devoured them.*
> [5] *Some fell on stony places, where they did not have much earth; and they immediately sprang up because they had no depth of earth.*
> [6] *But when the sun was up they were scorched, and because they had no root they withered away.*
> [7] *And some fell among thorns, and the thorns sprang up and choked them.*
> [8] *But others fell on good ground and yielded a crop: some a hundredfold, some sixty, some thirty.....*
> [18] *Therefore hear the parable of the sower:*
> [19] *When anyone hears the word of the kingdom, and does not understand it, then the wicked one comes and snatches away what was sown in his heart. This is he who received seed by the wayside.*
> [20] *But he who received the seed on stony places, this is he who hears the word and immediately receives it with joy;*
> [21] *yet he has no root in himself, but endures only for a while. For when tribulation or persecution arises because of the word, immediately he stumbles.*
> [22] *Now he who received seed among the thorns is he who hears the word, and the cares of this world and the deceitfulness of riches choke the word, and he becomes unfruitful.*
> [23] *But he who received seed on the good ground is he who hears the word and understands it, who indeed bears fruit and produces: some a hundredfold, some sixty, some thirty."*

Matthew 13:4-8, 18-23

Notice that the vast majority of the seeds sown did not produce result, not due to any fault of the seeds but because of the receptivity of the grounds in which they were sown. In other words, when the Word fails to produce the promised freedom, the problem is not with the Word but with the person. Jesus said the seed is like the Word of God (*Luke 8:11*) and the grounds are the different conditions of the hearers (*Luke 8:12-15*). Notice that every one of the three conditions of hearers that suffered a crop failure did not get to the stage of incubating the Word. Before the Word on the way side could be understood, the hearer got distracted by the preacher's tie and the day dream about Sunday lunch. The Word ended up being stolen by the devil. The seed on stony places was scorched when the hearer ran into a colleague who said, *"you are too educated to believe that kind of religious nonsense"*. The persecution gave no chance to the Word to gain root and interact with the ground.

The Word among thorns was choked by the preoccupation with working two *'full time'* jobs and one part time role in order to keep up with the Jones'. The Word lost the room needed to become intimate with the ground. Only the Word on good ground took the time to create the right atmosphere and make the right sacrifices to ensure that the Word thrived long enough to produce results.

Conquer your Fear

A failure to perceive the truth always perpetrates bondage and limitation. Following the death, burial and resurrection of Jesus, He made an appearance to Cleopas and another disciple on the Emmaus road (*Luke 24:13-35*). This was a time of extreme uncertainty about the personality, ministry and where about of Jesus. There were many unanswered questions. Was He really the Son of God as He claimed (*Matthew 26:63-64)*? If He was, how could the Son of God possibly die on the cross (*Matthew 27:40*)? How about the expectation that He was the coming deliverer of Israel (*Luke 24: 21*)? What about the claim that He would rise on the third day? It was now over three days and the grave was empty (*John 20:2*) but nobody knew His where about (*Luke 24:22-24*).

With all these questions unanswered, the disciples on

the way to Emmaus were bound by fear, sadness and confusion because 'their eyes were restrained, so that they did not **KNOW** Him' (Luke 24:14). They did not know Jesus, the **TRUTH** (John 14:6). They did not know the truth and this situation guaranteed their bondage. But the moment that 'their eyes were opened and they **knew** Him' (Luke 24:31) they broke lose of their fear and sadness. They became brand new persons. Their knowledge of the truth manufactured freedom from fear, timidity, sadness and confusion.

The same disciples who compelled Jesus to interrupt His journey and spend the night with them due to an apparent concern for 'His' safety, suddenly acquired the boldness to travel all the way back to Jerusalem on the same road, only now without Jesus' company. What had changed? Cleopas and the other disciple had come to know Him, the **Truth** and the knowledge of the **Truth** produced joy, boldness and hope. Your freedom is as close to you as the knowledge of the **Truth** that you discover.

Turn your Grief into Joy

Mary Magdalene had a similar experience at the resurrection tomb (John 20: 1-14). She arrived to an empty tomb on the third day after crucifixion and was perplexed by the experience. Apparently, the presence of two angels sitting at the head and foot of the tomb was not enough to soothe her grief on the loss of her Master. The angelic question could not seem to stop her weeping. When Jesus came on the scene, she failed to recognize Him and mistook Him for a gardener, who might help her to find her Master. Mary's grief and confusion came to an abrupt end when Jesus called her by name. She suddenly knew it was the Truth and the Truth freed her from her grief and confusion. An instant knowledge of the Truth terminated days of sorrow and gave way to ecstasy. Mary was so thrilled that it took an instruction from Jesus to stop her from jumping on Him in a bear hug. That is what knowledge of the Truth does. It transforms sorrow into joy, confusion into clarity and despair into hope.

Ride your Storm

Peter too had a similar revelation of the truth. His experience is recorded in *Matthew 14: 22-33*. This was just another day in the hectic ministry schedule of Jesus and His disciples. The disciples were with Jesus until He dispatched them in a boat and went for a private time of prayer. Around three in the morning, the situation on the sea became dire as the winds became contrary and the boat hit some high waves. To complicate matters, a water walking '*ghost*' was now making its way towards the boat.

The disciples were understandably perplexed and frightened. Jesus was absent, the sea was raging and a strange creature was heading towards them. The truth was that Jesus was the one walking on the sea but they did not know the Truth. The moment Peter recognized Jesus (*the Truth*), he became so bold that he requested an invitation to defy the laws of nature and walk on the very storm of which he was frightened moments before. Before you criticize Peter's loss of focus and the consequent near sinking experience, let me ask you how many times you have had the experience of taking one step on the local swimming pool? My point is that in a moment of knowing the Truth, Peter went from a man who was frightened of a storm to a man who walked on water. The fear of separation from his Master, sinking in a storm and being attacked by a ghost, all vanished in one moment of knowing the Truth.

Peter, Mary Magdalene and Cleopas all had one thing in common. They knew the Truth and the Truth manufactured their freedom from fear, confusion, sorrow and despair. The reality is that if the revealed Word of God is left to its own devices in your heart, it will always produce results (*Mark 4:26-29*). Therefore, your concern must be how to get a revelation of the Truth. One way of acquiring this dimension of knowledge of the Truth is by meditation.

Protected by Revelation

Let me share some personal experiences to show you how this works in practice. '*You defend us even when we are ignorant of an attack*' was a statement I found myself making often, a number of years ago. Although, you would not find a scripture with those precise words, references like *Psalms 91:1-2, 7-8* and *Psalm 34:7* express the same theme. I would spout the words out of my mouth ever so often without even thinking about it. I said it so often that it became part of my subconscious. I made the statement so often that it became a conviction in my heart that if I ever came under an attack, I did not need to be aware of it to experience divine deliverance.

One summer evening, I returned home to learn that the neighbour across the road had popped in to complain about my wife parking her car on his driveway. This seemed an extremely unlikely event and cheeky approach by the neighbour, until my wife went out to confirm the claim, to her utter disbelief. Somehow, the hand brake had disengaged and the car had rolled ten yards down our driveway coming to a halt neatly parked a few inches from the neighbour's car. The biggest miracle was not that there was no impact with the neighbour's car. The real cause for thanksgiving was that, this area was a favourite spot of *'hide and seek'* for local children who sometimes hid around the car especially in summer. I would not like to speculate about the possible outcome if this incident happened in the middle of one of those games. My confession had built a fortress of personal revelation, which brought deliverance even when we were unaware of the attack.

Let me close this chapter with a final illustration of this principle.

> [1] *Now faith is the substance of things hoped for, the evidence of things not seen.*
> [2] *For by it the elders obtained a good testimony*
>
> *Hebrews 11:1-2*

As I listened to those words on a Bible CD one morning, verse two seemed to leap out at me and lodge itself forcefully in my heart. Subsequently, I could not seem to get enough of this scripture. I found myself thinking about it and confessing it over myself over a period of time. At the end of the period, I discovered that about this time a critical decision on my direction in life and progress in ministry was being made, unknown to me. The decision was favourable. I indeed obtained a good report by faith.

Friend, if you will learn to unlock this dimension of operating by the truth that you know, in the revealed Word of God, you are about to permanently sever your relationship with long standing fear, confusion, sadness and despair and you are about to enter into a freedom that you have only dreamed about before now. Because the truth you know, guarantees your freedom.

CHAPTER SUMMARY

There are different degrees of knowledge of the truth in God's Word. Your degree of knowledge determines your degree of freedom

It is your responsibility to interact with God's Word until you come to an intimate knowledge of relevant truth for your situation because only an intimate knowledge of truth produces freedom

Every problem is an indication of an ignorance of relevant truth and no situation can withstand the force of a revealed Bible truth in the heart of a child of God

Chapter 6

Response Determines Reward

*D*oes it ever puzzle you that two Christians would attend the same service, sit in the same room, dance to the same worship music, give in the same offering plate, listen to the same message and one of them has a life changing encounter whilst the other leaves admiring the pastor's tie? There is a scriptural explanation for this mystery. Getting hold of this principle will change your attitude to the Word of God and your entire life forever. This principle relates to a certain facet of the operation and application of the Word of God.

The Bible teaches that Jesus, the Son of God and the Word of God in flesh (*John 1:14*) was anointed by the Holy Spirit without measure (*John 3:34*). In other words, Jesus was as anointed as anybody could ever be. It is impossible for any individual to carry a greater measure of anointing than Jesus carried during his earthly ministry. Since Jesus is the same, yesterday, today and forever (*Hebrews 13:8*), He would have been equally anointed on every single day of His earthly ministry. He was always as anointed as He ever was. That being the case, how come He got different results in different places where He ministered? How come some people received from this anointing and others didn't?

There is only one answer to the question. If the same degree of anointing on the same person produced different results in different individuals, the only variables are the individuals. The answer must lie with the individual recipients. We can only conclude that everyone received to the degree of their faith or cooperation with the ever constant flow of the anointing on Jesus. Look at the varying degree of results that Jesus obtained in three different places during His earthly ministry and you will see the point clearer.

Marched out of Town

28 When He had come to the other side, to the country of the Gergesenes, there met Him two demon-possessed men, coming out of the tombs, exceedingly fierce, so that no one could pass that way.

29 And suddenly they cried out, saying, "What have we to do with You, Jesus, You Son of God? Have You come here to torment us before the time?"

30 Now a good way off from them there was a herd of many swine feeding.

31 So the demons begged Him, saying, "If You cast us out, permit us to go away into the herd of swine."

32 And He said to them, "Go." So when they had come out, they went into the herd of swine. And suddenly the whole herd of swine ran violently down the steep place into the sea, and perished in the water.

33 Then those who kept them fled; and they went away into the city and told everything, including what had happened to the demon-possessed men.

³⁴ And behold, the whole city came out to meet Jesus. And when they saw Him, they begged Him to depart from their region.

Matthew 8:28-34

This is a strange account in the ministry of Jesus. The Son of God came to town and ran into two demoniacs. Up till this moment, these two guys had tormented the entire county; they had turned this part of town into a *'no-go'* area. The tomb or cemetery where they lived would have been disused. No one ever dared to take the route where these guys held sway. Jesus ran into them and instantly cast out the demons and restored the men to normality. In the process, an entire herd of pigs perished.

Right now, the mayor of Gergesenes ought to be hosting a citywide party! More importantly, somebody ought to be rounding up every mentally ill person in town and bringing them to the feet of Jesus for healing. Not so; the people were apparently upset that they had lost a herd of pigs. The income from the piggery was more important to them than the welfare and deliverance of two demon-possessed men. Therefore, they summarily marched Jesus out of town!

Isn't it amazing how some people really do not want a solution to their problems? They need the problem as a crutch to lean on. There are certain nations of the world, for example, where the corrupt political system sabotages and frustrates any candidate running for public office with an anti corruption agenda. The system likes the status quo because it guarantees illegitimate wealth and influence for the powers that be.

On a similar note, the story was told of a partially deaf man who was asked by the evangelist at the healing line, do you want to be healed. To the utter amazement of the preacher, the answer was no! On further enquiry, it transpired that, the deaf man had a nagging wife to whom he turned the deaf ear whenever the verbal rant began. Healing of the deaf ear would have taken away the remedy to the nagging problem, hence the man's preference for partial deafness. The Gergesenes apparently preferred to have the city tormented by demoniacs than to have their pigs perish in the sea with the offending demons. The demon possessed men had become a part of the city's profile and the people seemed to love it that way. How tragic!

A similar story repeats itself somewhere else in the Bible. How else can you explain the situation when Jesus walks up to a man who had been impotent for thirty eight years at the Pool of Bethesda, and asks *'do you want to be made whole'*? (*John 5:4-8*). The question seemed unnecessary and the answer seemed obvious, until the man opened his mouth and started to recount his life history of woes, when all that was needed was a *'yes'* or *'no'*. The thirty eight years of impotence had institutionalized the man. The problem had become an important part of his identity, to the point where he did not see a realistic future without it. Be careful not to idolize the situation you are dealing with to the point of elevating it to the central theme in your life.

Let's come back to the deliverance of the two men from Gergesenes. The hostile response of the region to the Word of God in flesh guaranteed that any further manifestation of deliverance or healing in the region was cut short. How can you experience healing after running the healer out of town? The same situation repeats itself in our pews and pulpits every Sunday when the written Word of God is preached. For various reasons, the response is hostile and this just truncates any manifestation of the power of God through His spoken word. Too many people leave the service exactly the way they came and then blame it on the preacher. They fail to realize that the manifestation of God's power is not just a function of what the preacher did or did not do but also a function of their cooperation with the power of God on the message and the preacher.

Carpenter or Great Physician

Let's look at another situation in *Mark 6: 1-6*:

> ¹ *Then He went out from there and came to His own country, and His disciples followed Him.*
> ² *And when the Sabbath had come, He began to teach in the synagogue. And many hearing Him were astonished, saying, "Where did this Man get these things? And what wisdom is this which is given to Him, that such mighty works are performed by His hands!*
> ³ *Is this not the carpenter, the Son of Mary, and brother of James, Joses, Judas, and Simon? And are not His sisters here with us?" And they were offended at Him.*
> ⁴ *But Jesus said to them, "A prophet is not without honor except in his own country, among his own relatives, and in his own house.*
> ⁵ *And he could there do no mighty work, save that he laid his hands upon a few sick folk, and healed them.*
> ⁶ *And he marveled because of their unbelief. And he went round about the villages, teaching.*

Mark 6: 1-6

A similar account of resistance to Jesus' ministry is given in *Mark 6:1-6*. Jesus returned to His home town of Nazareth and met with untold resistance. Somehow, the Son of God came to town but the Nazarenes saw the son of Mary. The Great Physician was passing by but all the people could see was the return of the carpenter who grew up down the road. The only begotten Son of God was visiting, but they only saw the brother of James, Joses, Judas and Simon. The Nazarenes gave Jesus the cold shoulder and ended up short-circuiting the anointing on Him. In actual fact they deliberately tuned Him out, so they could not receive. The attitude of the people and their lack of receptivity constituted a hindrance to the anointing on Jesus. As a result, He could do no mighty works, except heal a few sick people.

Notice, that the ministry of Jesus, the very Son of God was incapacitated by the receptivity of the people. He *'could'* do no mighty works. That means that even if He tried, on this occasion, He couldn't. If the familiarity of the people of Nazareth, limited the power of God from flowing through the unlimited anointing on the Word of God in flesh, how much more is the familiarity of the people of God with the preacher, limiting the anointing upon God's spoken Word from producing the desired effect in our pews and pulpit today? We all have a responsibility never to allow our familiarity with the preacher to breed contempt for his/her message.

Recognition and Reward

Look at another event in *Matthew 14: 34-36:*

> [34] *When they had crossed over, they came to the land of Gennesaret.*
> [35] *And when the men of that place **recognized** Him, they sent out into all that surrounding region, brought to Him all who were sick,*
> [36] *and begged Him that they might only touch the hem of His garment. And as many as touched it were made perfectly well.*
>
> *Matthew 14: 34-36*

The people of Gennesaret were different from the folks in Gergesenes and Nazareth. Notice how Gennesaret responded to the Son of God. First, they recognized Him. As whom did they recognize Him? Their actions demonstrated what recognition they gave Him. They recognized Him as the Great Physician, as the omnipotent

Son of God, as the Messenger of God of the hour, sent to them for deliverance. They recognized Jesus as the Word of God in Flesh. They recognized Jesus and sent messages to all the surrounding regions that sick persons should be brought to Him. Their expectation was at an all time high.

The recognition provoked a strong manifestation of the power of God to the point that the sick only needed to touch the hem of Jesus' garment to be healed. Everyone who made the touch received a touch. There was a hundred percent success rate. Can you imagine the transformation that the right attitude to the Word of God in flesh made on an entire region? I suspect that the health care job market was thrown into a crisis in this region. Since all the sick people in that region had been brought to Jesus and as many of them that touched the hem of His garment had been made perfectly well, the health care practitioners in the region would have become jobless. The doctors, nurses, physiotherapists and opticians in this region would have run out of business.

Why would you need a doctor when all the flu, headaches, heart problems, kidney failure, liver cirrhosis, high blood pressure, skin rashes, depression, alcohol dependence and substance misuse addictions were all healed? Gennesaret became the healthiest region in Israel by the time Jesus left, all because of the attitude of the people. The people were not only healed, they were perfectly healed and '*perfectly well*'. That's my own idea of healing! How about you?

All three regions of Gargasenes, Nazareth and Gennesaret had the opportunity of one visit each, from the same preacher, under the same unlimited measure of the anointing, in the same country, but all three regions obtained different results. What was different? ...The cities and the response of the people to the manifested presence of Jesus, the revealed Word of God. (*Revelation 19:13*). Gergesenes and Nazareth ended up with a few healings and Gennesaret ended up as the healthiest city in the nation.

Obviously, the response of the hearer to the Word of God greatly affects the result that is produced. Don't bother going to a meeting if you don't respect the preacher and believe that you can receive something from him or her. This is a dimension of the operation and application of the Word of God that is alien to many Christians. Let us conclude this chapter with these pieces of practical advice. If you will benefit maximally from any exposure to the Word of God you need to take a few practical steps:

- Recognize the written Word of God for what it is-this held the key to the landslide success that Gennesaret experienced.

- Treat the written Word with the same regard you would give to Jesus if He stepped into the room in person

- Refuse to get offended. Offence was the stumbling block for the folks in Gergesenes and Nazareth.

CHAPTER SUMMARY

The result you obtain from your exposure to the Word
of God is as much dependent on you as it depends on
the preacher

You must recognise, revere and receive the Word of God
in order to produce results from the Word

Offence is a stumbling block to receiving any result
from the application of God's Word

Chapter 7

God's Word in 3D

*G*od's Word in 3D! From where did that come? Is this just another fancy title or a valid Bible concept? Let's find out.

God of Many Parts: Father, Son and Holy Spirit

14And God said to Moses, "I AM WHO I AM." And He said, "Thus you shall say to the children of Israel, 'I AM has sent me to you.' "

Exodus 3:14

God is a many sided being. Surely, you know about the Father, the Son and the Holy Spirit (*Matthew 28:19*). We call all three of them God (*1 John 5:7*) but each of these have different personalities. God is a God of many parts. Look at the pages of the Bible and convince yourself. Moses, Elijah, Isaiah and Abraham all stood out as servants of God. Each of these men encountered God at one point in their lives or another. When God showed Himself to Moses in a burning bush (*Exodus 3:2*) He introduced Himself as 'I AM

WHO I AM' (*Exodus 3:14*). '*I am who? What does that mean?* ' Bible expositors have said, that God was simply telling Moses: '*what you need is what I am*'. Let me say that in 3D language: '*I am many sided. When my people are in bondage in Egypt, I show up as 'I Am the Deliverer' (Exodus 3:8)*''. When they run out of water in the wilderness, I come on the scene as '*I Am the Provider*' (*Exodus 17:1-7*). *When they confront a Red Sea that is too vast to cross and an Egyptian army that is to too strong to resist, I put on my combat gear and come on the scene as 'I Am the Mighty Man of War'* (*Exodus 14:28-15:3; Isaiah 42:13*). '*Take your pick Moses; whatever you need me to be I AM*'. I feel a shout coming on just writing that. What a God, we serve!

I grew up in Nigeria where the local gods had specialities: god of harvest, god of thunder, god of iron! The trouble was if your chosen god was god of thunder, you could not approach him with a crop failure issue; you need the god of harvest for that. If yours was the god of iron, you could not solicit him for a weather problem. No, that is an issue for the god of thunder. That meant you needed to have several gods, one for every eventuality of life. I am so thankful that Jehovah, the many-sided one that we serve does not have such limitations. He will fix your character, health, your finances and your relationships all in one swipe. Glory to His name!

Let us return to Elijah, Isaiah and Abraham. When it came time to speak to Elijah, God chose a still small voice (*1 Kings 19:12-13*). Isaiah also heard a voice, but it was neither still, nor small. The scene was very different. There was smoke; there were scary creatures and the voice was so forceful that it shook the pillars of the door (*Isaiah 6:1-6*). Isaiah saw Him as the Lord of Hosts and the High and Lifted One. How about God's encounter with Abraham? Did he see a burning bush? No! Was it a repeat of the door shaking voice? No. Instead, Abraham entertained Him as a visitor (*Genesis 18:1-21*). These are all different manifestations of a many-sided God.

How about Jesus, the Son of God and the express image of the Father (*John 14:9, Hebrews 1:2-3*)? Watch the Son of God in action and notice how He functioned on several levels in different aspects of His earthly ministry. Sometimes we saw Him operate as a spirit being. Come with me and let us take a quick trip to the scene on that fateful day in *Mark 2:1-12*. Jesus was holding a private meeting in a crowded house. Five men turned up and tried to enter but could not gain entry, at least not through the door. Suddenly, the roof started rattling and the next thing you knew: these desperate men were in the middle of breaking into the meeting, not through the door, but through the roof! That was not all. One of these gatecrashers was bed bound from paralysis. By instinct Jesus, knew the cause of the sickness was sin. He pronounced forgiveness over the paralysed man and in an instant, the man picked up the bed he '*rode*' into the meeting, completely healed.

At the same time, Jesus knew in '*His Spirit*' that the religious leaders in the meeting were upset about His pronouncement: '*Who does He think He is, to make such statements? Only God can forgive sin. Is He trying to make Himself equal with God?*' Clearly, you can see Jesus' Spirit in operation in this account. Now take a short leap forward in history, with me, to the crucifixion story. Jesus was hanging on the cross and just before taking His last breath at Calvary, He declared, "*Father, into your hands I commit my spirit*" (*Luke 23:33, 46*). Did you see the point? Jesus functioned and knew things by His Spirit during these encounters.

His Spirit is only one aspect of His being that we see in manifestation in the Bible. At the age of twelve, He engaged the scholars of His time in an intellectual conversation and reasoned in the temple (*Luke 2:42-48*). Here we see Him functioning as an intelligent being. After forty days of fasting, He became hungry (*Luke 4:2*), a natural response of the human body. Therefore, Jesus was spirit, soul and body in His make up.

Think about this for a moment. Jesus, the Lamb of God (*John 1:29*) is also Jesus, the Lion of Judah (*Revelation 5:5*). Take a close look at His ministry; it also has many aspects. He is a Teacher, Pastor, Evangelist, Prophet and Apostle all rolled into one. He was fondly called Teacher or Rabbi during His earthly ministry (*Matthew 23:8; John 3:2*). In *John 10:2 and Hebrews 13:20* we see Him, as Jesus the Pastor and Shepherd of the Sheep. Join Him on the road as He pursues His evangelistic ministry through the towns and cities of first century Palestine (*Matthew 4:23; 9:35*). Sit in the pew in the temple in Nazareth, listen to His first public sermon as He declares: *The Spirit of the Lord has anointed me to be a preacher of good news; I am an evangelist (Luke 4:18-19, paraphrased)*. He called Himself a prophet (*Matthew 13:57*) and the people of His days recognised Him as one (*Matthew 14:5*). He is the Apostle of our faith and the High Priest of our calling (*Hebrews 3:1*). Can you see that even His ministry had many sides?

His relationships were also on multiple levels. He had spiritual relationships with God His heavenly Father and the Holy Spirit His Helper (*Matthew 3:16-17; John 3:34-35, Luke 3:22*). Peek into His ancestral home in Nazareth and learn about His relationships with Mary and His siblings (*Mark 6:3*). How about His business relationships? After all, He was a carpenter (*Mark 6:1-3*); somebody must have bought the furniture He made! He had social contact with the people of His home town and was friends with Lazarus, Mary and Martha (*John 11; John 12:1*). Do not think for a moment that all those relationships were friendly either! Friendly, is not the way I would describe His relationships with opponents like the Pharisees and Sadducees (*Matthew 22:23-46*).

Love in 3D

¹⁷ That Christ may dwell in your hearts through faith; that you, being rooted and grounded in love,
¹⁸ may be able to comprehend with all the saints what is the width and length and depth and height—
¹⁹ to know the love of Christ which passes knowledge; that you may be filled with all the fullness of God

Ephesians 3: 17-19

The nature and relationships of the Son of God are not the only many-sided aspects of His being. You may know about 3D imagery, 3D movies and 3D glasses, but have you heard of 3D love? Paul tells us in his letter to the Ephesians that even the love of Jesus is multilayered. It has the elements of length, depth and height. In fact, in the true sense of the term, His love is 3D (three-dimensional).

Multi-dimensional Spirit

We see this same multidimensional attributes in the Holy Spirit, the third person of the God Head. He is also multifaceted. At creation, He hovered over the formless, void and dark waters and brought light and order (*Genesis 1:1-3*). He alighted like a dove on Jesus at the Jordan River (*Luke 3:22*); and on the Day of Pentecost He came to rest on the one hundred and twenty disciples like tongues of fire (*Acts 2:1-4*). In the book of Revelation, He manifested

Himself in the form of the seven Spirits of God (*Revelation 4:5, 5:6*). These are just a few examples of the multiple aspects of the Holy Spirit's nature. We could go on, but I think we have made the point that all three personalities of the God Head are many sided in their nature and attributes.

God and His Many-Sided Word

Do not bother trying; you cannot separate God and His Word. They are one and the same (*John 1:1*). God is His Word and the Word of God is God. No wonder Jesus, the second person of the Godhead is called the Word of God (*Revelation 19:13*). Since God is many sided, His Word is invariably multidimensional. This is your first proof in this study that God's Word is multidimensional. Therefore, you would be completely in line with scripture to say that the Word of God is multifaceted. Let us say it this way: the Bible's testimony about itself is that God's Word is multidimensional.

Multi-dimensional Wisdom

Now we know that God, His nature and His manifestations are many-sided. What other aspect of Him has multiple parts? Take His wisdom for example.

> [10] *to the intent that now the manifold wisdom of God might be made known by the church to the principalities and powers in the heavenly places*
>
> *Ephesians 3:10*

The wisdom of God too has many facets. Not one, two, three or a few facets, but many. The word '*manifold*' simply means many folds. That paints a word picture in the mind, doesn't it? When you go on a trip you neatly fold your clothes into a suitcase. Just because the cloths are folded, you are able to pack more into the suitcase than you would, if you just tried to stuff them in ruffled. When you arrive at your destination you unpack your suitcase. First you open the suitcase and access the compartments. You work through the layers of clothing and then you unfold each item of clothing. At this point you only have a view of the cloths on the surface but as you work through the layers of clothing you begin to access the cloths in the depths of your suitcase which could not be seen from the surface. Imagine someone else like your mum or spouse packed the suitcase. The more you unpack, the more you see the depth of thought that was put into the task. That is a picture of the wisdom of God. So the wisdom of God needs to be unravelled because it is in many folds. The more of His wisdom that you unpack, the more of it you discover. The discovery of one dimension is not the end but only an entrance to another dimension. We can never reach the end of His wisdom (*Romans 11:33*) because His understanding is unsearchable (*Isaiah 40:28*).

> [10] *[The purpose is] that through the church the complicated, many-sided wisdom of God in all its infinite variety and innumerable aspects might now be made known to the angelic rulers and authorities (principalities and powers) in the heavenly sphere*
>
> Ephesians 3:10 (AMP)

The Amplified version of *Ephesians 3:10* sheds even more light on the many-sided nature of this wisdom. It is of infinite variety and of innumerable aspects. In other words, it is multidimensional. Orologists specialise in the study of mountains. They tell us that these huge landmarks occupy such large land masses that the different *"sides"* of the same mountain may lay in different cities, regions or even nations. Mountains can create multiple climates and varied vegetations in their immediate locality. Each side of the mountain generally creates a unique vegetation and climatic condition, which might be significantly different from those created by other sides. Two persons observing the same mountain from different sides could end up describing two completely opposite albeit accurate climates and vegetation. Similarly, God's wisdom has multiple sides and each side is unique in its character. The way we get the full benefit of His wisdom is to access its many varieties. Just like, the way to fully appreciate the character of a mountain is to see its numerous sides.

Resourceful Wisdom

The Psalmist says God's Words are to be desired above gold (*Psalms 19:9-11*). This is because every nugget of God's wisdom is precious. It is full of multiple resources. Let me illustrate this from the human body. Make a fist with your right hand. Now, look at your fist. Your kidney is about the size of that fist. Can you imagine that each of your kidneys contains about 37 miles (60 Kilometers) of tubes[1]? That is enough tube to span the length of six hundred and fifty football fields. Think about that for a moment. How can tubes that long fit into a structure that small? This is only possible because the tubes are neatly folded. In the same way there is so much resourcefulness in every nugget of God's wisdom because it is in multiple folds. God can afford to pack so much resource in just one nugget of wisdom because His wisdom is folded in multiples. You could look upon God's wisdom as a neatly folded resource pack.

You may ask, '*what has all this got to do with me?*' We must all learn to obey the Word of God even when there is no logic to it. Obey anyway, because what seems illogical from your point of view may make perfect sense if you were to see things from another angle.

There is another application. The wisdom of God is in many folds and these folds could take time to unravel. Sometimes it takes years. This is the reason why sometimes we do not get results from following God's Words because we did not follow the process through and we gave up before the wisdom totally unfolded. God may be asking you to show kindness to somebody who is being nasty to you now. You have tried being kind but the more you tried, the more nasty the person got. Do not give up. Many years down the line, that same person may hold the key to your progress and this time she would be a changed person and would decide to repay you for your kindness.

God's Word is God's Wisdom

God's wisdom is in His Word. In fact, you could describe God's wisdom as being the same thing as His Word. This is how Solomon describes the connection in the book of Proverbs: *'Get wisdom, Get understanding! Do not forget, nor turn away from the words of my mouth'* (*Proverbs 4:5*). *My son, pay attention to my wisdom, listen well to my words of insight* (*Proverbs 5:1 NIV*). According to these scriptures, the Words that come out of God's mouth are the very essence of wisdom.

Wisdom comes from what God says. It is impossible to acquire God's wisdom without first listening to what He has to say. God's Word is simply impregnated with His wisdom. It is impossible to have one and not the other. God's wisdom comes from God's Word and God's Word is full of God's wisdom. Since God's wisdom is His Word and His wisdom is multidimensional, then it is in line with the scripture, if we declare that His Word too is multidimensional. This is our second proof from scripture that God's Word is multidimensional.

Jesus: Word of God, Wisdom of God

²³ But we preach Christ crucified, to the Jews a stumbling block and to the Greeks foolishness;
²⁴ but to those who are called, both Jews and Greeks, Christ the power of God and the wisdom of God.

1 Corinthians 1:23-24

Jesus is not only the Word of God; He is also the wisdom of God. You could say that Christ is the wisdom of God in manifestation or the wisdom of God in flesh. We have already seen that Jesus is multifaceted in His nature and that the wisdom of God is many sided. We have also seen that Christ is the Word of God and that the wisdom of God is the Word of God. Now we see that Jesus is the wisdom of God. If Jesus Christ is the Word of God and He is also the Wisdom of God, and the Wisdom of God is multisided; it should be easy to accept that the Word of God is also multisided. This is the third premise that demonstrates that the Word of God is multisided.

Let me conclude with a summary of the main thoughts of this chapter. God is a God of many parts. The Father, Son and Holy Spirit are multidimensional. Jesus is the Word of God and the Wisdom of God. God's Wisdom is His Word. Since God is many-sided and God is His own Word, then the Word of God is also many sided. The wisdom of God is many-sided and the wisdom of God is the Word of God, so the Word of God too is many-sided. Finally, Jesus is the Word and Wisdom of God. Since He is multisided, the Word of God too is multisided.

Page | 88

CHAPTER SUMMARY

God's Word cannot be separated from His being, His wisdom and His Love; and all three are many-sided

The Godhead is many-sided in make-up, ministry and manifestation

The many-sided nature of God's Word and wisdom makes them limitless in resources

Chapter 8

Meditation Unveiled[1]

*I*n contemporary society, the term *'meditation'* conveys a variety of meanings to different people. An ancient eastern practice which requires the practitioner to adopt awkward postures whilst focussing his or her mind on abstract thoughts, is the picture that some see at the mention of the word. Others think of a kind of martial art or a practice like yoga in relation to the term. Some even connect the term with more contemporary concepts like Neuro Linguistic Programming (*NLP*).

Recently I met a woman who had been on an NLP seminar. She recounted her experience of participating in an exercise, which required her to walk bare footed and blindfolded. She emerged at the end of the task needing to rinse her soiled feet. Contrary to the instructor's claim about the temperature of the water, the woman insisted that the water was warm, not cold. It turned out that the water was indeed cold. The perception of warmth was because, unknown to the woman, she had just walked barefooted over a live bed of hot coal. She felt no discomfort, was not hurt and was not even aware of the danger until after the exercise.

How could a human being achieve such a feat? Prior to the exercise the instructor, without disclosing the details of the task, had verbally brainwashed the delegates into believing that they could complete the next task almost effortlessly, just by setting their mind to it and by repeatedly telling themselves out loud that they could do it. The delegates had no idea what they were getting into.

So, does meditation have a place in Christianity and does the scripture have anything to say about its practice? The resounding answer to both questions is yes. We have already spent a number of chapters focussing on the nature of God's Word. It is now time to turn attention to the operations of God's Word. The first dimension of the operation of God's Word we will consider is meditation. Welcome to meditation in 3D!

Muse and Mutter

What do you mean by meditation? *Meditation simply means to ponder, to consider intently, to muse over, to think on, or to mutter certain thoughts repeatedly.* This is how God explained it to Joshua:

> [8] *This Book of the Law shall not depart from your mouth, but you shall meditate in it day and night, that you may observe to do according to all that is written in it. For then you will make your way prosperous, and then you will have good success.*
>
> *Joshua 1:8*

In this short passage, God gives Joshua the secret of success through meditation and conversely the mystery of failure.

Let us summarise what He said:

- The book of the law shall not depart from your mouth- what you SAY
- You shall meditate on it day and night-what you THINK
- You will observe to do what is written in it-what you DO
- Then you will prosper and have good success- what you BECOME

Meditation is the sum total of what you say and think, which in turn affects what you do and become. The ultimate goal of meditation is to shape the person that you become. The person that you become depends on the things that you do. We have a divine guarantee that acting upon or doing the Word of God always produces a blessing (*Psalms 1:1-3; James 1:25*). *'That is precisely the problem'*, you may say. *I know that if I can somehow get myself to act on the Word of God, my problems are by gone! But, I cannot seem to muster the effort to act on the word. I want to practise the word but it is a struggle.*

If that is your plight, I have good news for you. Notice the two critical transitions in *Joshua 1:8*.The power to succeed is in doing (*that you may observe to do…for then, you will make your way prosperous*) and the power to do is in meditation (*you shall meditate in it; Why? that you may observe to do*). The key to doing the Word of God is meditating on it. In order words, do not preoccupy yourself with the pressure to be a doer of the Word. You just see to it that you meditate on the Word and without even realising it; meditation will produce the power to do and act on the Word.

Take care of meditation and meditation will take care of the motivation and motivation will take care of the capacity to act on the Word.

Meditation is a means to doing or acting on the Word of God. Meditation is not the ultimate but a means to the ultimate. The power to do the Word comes from meditation. Meditation generates the spiritual stamina that you need to put the Word of God into practice. The formula is simple: Mediate, Do, Succeed.

Brainwashing

Do not kid yourself; your meditation will eventually play out in spontaneous behaviour. Teenagers and youth beware! You cannot listen to music, which encourages irresponsible sexual behaviour, drugs and criminal activity all day long, and expect to live a life free of sexual misconduct and drug abuse. The common lie is to tell yourself that the lyrics don't matter, only the rhythm. There is a growing body of scientific evidence that your thoughts and actions are influenced by the words you hear and speak. It is not as difficult as you might think. Psychiatrist Louis B. Cady, MD., is an authority on the subject. His work has shown that the words and thoughts you constantly allow to linger in your subconscious mind produce a kind of *'self brainwashing*[2]*'* . Tolerated for long enough, views and ideas, which you did not initially believe to be true, gradually become accepted as truth and perceived as acceptable ways of thinking. If this can happen, with secular music, how much more can the Word of God produce a similar but more powerful effect?

This is good news. Do not preoccupy yourself with trying to believe what God's Word says about you at the outset. You just listen to it, and recite it and think about it long enough and before you know it, you will believe it. This powerful idea plays itself out everyday around you. You just have not thought about it. Let me illustrate it.

Public speaking has been a part of my job for many years. This means that I am constantly telling stories, using anecdotes and recounting experiences to my audiences. Some of these illustrations are real and others are imaginary (*parables*). After many years of using some of these parables, I got to a point where they became so real to me that I genuinely struggled to tell the difference between the real and the imaginary stories. I would start to tell a story as though it really happened and in the middle I would stop and say *"I honestly do not remember if this did happened or if it is just an imaginary story to illustrate my point"*. Such is the power of meditation.

Meditation or Study

Meditation is not the same as reading or studying large portions of the Word of God at a sitting. Meditation means picking out a few verses or even a few phrases in a verse and pondering and turning it/them over in your mind over a period. On the contrary, studying the Word means that you read portions (sometimes large portions) of it with the intention of understanding, assimilating and retaining the information.

Look at a few contrasts between meditating and studying the Word. Meditation produces stamina to act, but study produces information to act upon. So meditation without study is like an athlete who has built up plenty of stamina but does not have the necessary technique for her event. On the other hand, study without meditation is like this same athlete, having the technical know-how but lacking the stamina to practice what she knows to do. In both cases, her success would be limited. In the first instance, due to poor technique and in the second case due to lack of stamina. You must learn to meditate and study the word side by side. Meditation gives depth of insight but study gives breath of insight.

Meditation is a process of feeding yourself with God's Word with the intention of assimilating it. Meditation and study are two separate but complementary activities. They are similar but not mutually exclusive. In other words, neither of these can be substituted for the other. You get the best results when you combine both. In recent years, I have experienced unprecedented spiritual growth. This growth was directly due to my discovery of the link between meditation and studying. Until then, despite being a Christian for decades, I had focussed entirely on studying the Word of God. My discovery of the art of meditation radically transformed my time in the Word and my entire life.

How to Meditate

The obvious question to ask is this: If meditation holds the key to my doing the Word, which in turn is the secret of success, how exactly should I meditate on the Word? Here are a few practical tips to help you start out.

Repetitive Meditation

One of the most important keys to successful meditation is repetition. Ironically, the reason why meditation is so powerful is also the very reason why many Christians avoid it. We live at a time and age in which we are spoiled for choice on everything. As a result, most people are consumed with an endless quest to try something new.

This consumer mentality affects every aspect of life. In certain parts of the world, it would take you over a year to watch all the TV channels available on your subscription, if you watched a new one everyday. Even something as ordinary as getting a cup of coffee can become a laborious process when confronted with dozens of varieties to choose from in a branded coffee outlet. You could have a Cappuccino, or a Latte, or Mocha. Then you must decide whether you want it with cream or without cream. Whilst you are at it, do not forget to state whether you want it decaffeinated or not; and one final thing, do you want it tall or grande?. Those of us who live in the West have tried buying a mobile phone, researching a subject on the Internet, or even buying a loaf of bread from a large supermarket. The one lesson we have all learnt from these experiences is: be clear in your mind what you really want before you start out. Otherwise, you will end up completely confused by the variety of options presented to you.

The challenge is to want to try as many of the options as possible and this forces you to change from one option to another in the course of time. There is a tendency for this attitude to become a habit, which affects your general outlook to life. The outcome is that people get bored so easily, their attention span becomes very short and they develop a craving for constant variety and change in activity. You then introduce the subject of Bible meditation, which requires pondering and mulling over the same scripture repeatedly in your mind over a period and the hyperactive mind automatically switches off. This is the challenge!

God has set meditation up to be a repetitive reflective process. There is nothing we can do to change that. Why would we want to change something from the way the all-wise God has set it up in the first place anyway? There are good reasons why meditation is repetitive. Repetition creates intensity. It sharpens focus and brings clarity. God does not always make sense to the human mind but the subject of meditation is one thing on which He does make plenty of sense. Think about it, any practice that helps you to increase your intensity, focus and clarity is bound to enhance your capacity for success. Meditation does exactly that and little wonder it holds the key to success. After all, no indecisive person ever achieved success.

> [11] *God hath spoken once; twice have I heard this; that power belongeth unto God.*
>
> *Psalm 62:11(KJV)*

We can learn a whole lot of wisdom from David's proclamation in *Psalm 62:11*. If God only spoke once, how come David heard it twice? I suggest that first David heard God speak and then he put what God said in his own mouth and repeated it to himself so that he could hear it a second time. This is a powerful key to applying the Word of God. If you will ever become all that God said about you, you will need to learn to hear what God said more than once by repeating it to yourself until it becomes so much a part of your sub-consciousness and your reality. This is what meditation is all about.

Let us look at another practical requirement of meditation.

Daily Meditation

In *Joshua 1:8*, which I quoted earlier, God told Joshua that meditation must be done by day and by night. This is a figurative reference to a daily activity. A day and a night cycle refer to a 24-hour period. Meditation is not something you can afford to practice occasionally or randomly. It must be done daily. There is something powerful about pondering and muttering the Word of God to your self on a daily basis. I once heard a preacher say that the Word of God has a long-term effect on the human spirit. I know of no better way to expose the human spirit to the long-term effect of the Word than to meditate the word daily.

Meditating on the Word daily saturates your entire being with the power of God in a way that nothing else does. There is something about a daily dose of meditation that builds a reserve of God's Word in your heart. Maintaining this kind of discipline over a period of time will build up an awesome edifice of the Word of God in your life.

In September 2008, I had the privilege of visiting the Petronas Twin Towers in Kuala Lumpur. At 88 stories tall, this modern architectural masterpiece remains an envy of many nations, and an imposing beauty to behold. 41 stories above street level, I walked the sky bridge which links the two towers. It is difficult to behold this wonder of the modern world without asking how long it took to build. It only took 5 years from conception to occupancy! How is this possible? Work was done on the project every single day. It is amazing how much you can achieve just by working consistently on a project every day for several years. If human effort can achieve such outstanding results through daily effort over several years, how much more can the consistent application of God's Word through daily meditation produce in your life?

Jesus said that man shall not live by bread alone but by every Word that comes out of God's mouth (*Matthew 4: 4*). He later taught His disciples to pray, our Father who is in heaven...give us this day our daily bread. Bread, in this context, refers not only to physical food but also spiritual nourishment. The message is simple; both physical and spiritual food must be taken daily.

Focussed Meditation

In his letter to Timothy, the young pastor and protégé, Paul, gives more practical advice about meditation. In verse fifteen, of chapter four we read, *'Meditate on these things; give yourself entirely to them, that your progress may be evident to all'*. Paul's admonition was that Timothy should meditate on his mentor's words and give himself entirely to the subject of his meditation. Let me paraphrase Paul's words, *'Timothy, don't do your meditation half heartedly, give it all you've got; give it your very best shot; focus on it; don't be absent-minded about it. Do not be laid back about meditation. Take meditation seriously, address it head on'*.

If you have ever tried meditating on God's Word, and have done it daily for any amount of time, you would understand the relevance of Paul's words to Timothy. One of the greatest challenges to fruitful meditation is absent-mindedness. When you have repeated the same thought to yourself dozens of times for several minutes daily over a period of time, it becomes difficult to avoid going into auto pilot mode. However, Paul says to Timothy, and to you *'remain focussed'*; do not allow your mind to drift; remain completely alert. Do not slip into daydreaming! If you must daydream, let it be about the subject of your meditation. Let the dream be about you seeing yourself in the reality of what you are meditating.

Focus is not only about the state of your mind. It is also about the material you meditate on. With a Bible that contains thirty one thousand, one hundred and seventy three verses spread over one thousand one hundred and eighty nine chapters compiled in sixty six books, you are right to ask, *'where on earth do I start?'* I know from experience that meditation produces the best results when you select a small number of issues to focus on during your meditation time. You will get better results if you give yourself entirely to meditating on a few priority areas at any one time than if you try to diffuse your efforts by spreading your meditation time too thin across several subjects.

Of all the issues that you are dealing with, decide which two or three are the most pressing and concentrate your meditation efforts on them. The issue may be anger, impatience, selfishness, bitterness, un-forgiveness, poor health, debt, marital problems, or the job. What is your area of most pressing need or defeat? Find suitable scriptures that answer the need and meditate on them until you experience positive change. Give yourself entirely to seeing the situation change in these few areas. Devote your meditation time almost exclusively to these selected areas and in due time your progress will be seen, not just by you, not just by others, but by all.

I recently heard the story of Dr. C. Thomas Anderson. In his book, *'Becoming a Millionaire God's Way'*, he testified about the transforming power of the Word of God. After Dr. Anderson recognised that if he did not get proactive on his attack on poverty, he was going to end up being a victim of the generational poverty that had plagued his family for several generations. He wrote out all prosperity scriptures in the Bible, dictated them in his own voice on an audio recording and made copies, which played 24 hours in his home, car, and bedroom and that of his wife. No wonder generational poverty gave way to generational wealth in Dr Anderson's life.

CHAPTER SUMMARY

The key to success in life is to SAY, THINK and DO the Word of God until you BECOME what the Word of God says

Studying and meditating on God's Word are two different things and both activities must be combined to benefit fully from the Word of God

The key to meditation is daily, repetitive focussed speaking and thinking about the Word of God until it becomes a part of your subconscious

Chapter 9

The Power of Repetition

9 pointed out in the last chapter that one of the most important applications of the Word of God is to repeat it to yourself, over and over again. Let us turn our attention to this dimension of the operation of the Word of God and see this through our 3D glasses. We see the principle in the ministry of Jesus time and again. Jesus was also into repetition. One of the phrases that Jesus used often to emphasise important points was *'verily, verily (John 1:51; 3:3; 5:19*). He used the same phrase over twenty times in the gospels. Why did Jesus have to say *'verily, verily'*? Why did He not just say, 'verily, I say'? Repetition brings emphasis, and one way that Jesus emphasised an important point was by using this phrase. Repeating God's Word to yourself in meditation will cause the Word to impact your heart in a way that no other discipline can produce.

> *[15] So when they had eaten breakfast, Jesus said to Simon Peter, Simon, son of Jonah do you love Me more than these?*
> *He said to Him, "Yes, Lord; You know that I love You." He said to him, "Feed My lambs."*

¹⁶ He said to him again a second time, "Simon, son of Jonah, do you love Me?" He said to Him, "Yes, Lord; You know that I love You." He said to him, "Tend My sheep."
¹⁷ He said to him the third time, "Simon, son of Jonah, do you love Me?" Peter was grieved because He said to him the third time, "Do you love Me?" And he said to Him, "Lord, You know all things; You know that I love You." Jesus said to him, "Feed My sheep.
¹⁸ Most assuredly, I say to you, when you were younger, you girded yourself and walked where you wished; but when you are old, you will stretch out your hands, and another will gird you and carry you where you do not wish."

John 21: 15-18

The above scripture is an interesting account of one of the last conversations between Jesus and Peter before Jesus ascended into heaven. Before we discuss the content of the conversation, I want you to see the context. Jesus has just spent three and a half years of ministry pouring His life into twelve of His staff. His intention is that after His physical departure from the earth, these men are going to carry on spreading the gospel to the uttermost parts of the earth (*Mark 16:15, Acts 1:8*). Do not forget that at this time the gospel has only reached Israel and its borders. This is a huge task to commit onto just twelve men. These men must take the gospel forward; they must develop the movement that Jesus started into a global phenomenon. You need men who are dedicated, resolute and energetic for such a task.

Things are not looking promising on the surface, because just before the climax of His earthly ministry (*the crucifixion, death, and resurrection*) one of these men deserts to the enemy camp and commits suicide (*Matthew 27:3-5*). Now, Jesus is resurrected and is making an unscheduled appearance to the disciples at the Sea of Tiberias. The only other problem is that, at this time the remaining eleven men seem to have given up on the mission within a few days of the master's *'departure'*. Peter, the de facto leader of the group, floated an idea about making a career move back to his former occupation, fishing, and the others have bought into the idea.

Notice that Jesus essentially asked Peter the same question three times. Was Jesus just being pedantic or what? Why would Jesus repeat a question over and over when Peter's answer was essentially the same on every occasion? Well, despite all that has been said, a second look at the context of this conversation would reveal the gravity of the situation and the keen emphasis on the question. Anyone of us who has an iota of discernment should pay attention when the Son of God repeats a question three times. Jesus is not a gainsayer and He is not into vain repetition, therefore if He says it three times, there must be something important here.

The clue lies in a look into Peter's world. At this point in time, the events of the last many days had just thrown Peter's world into a state of flux. He was not alone in this predicament. All the remaining ten disciples were in the same situation. Jesus, their master; Jesus, their hero; Jesus, their employer; Jesus, their mentor; Jesus, their leader, had just been crucified and buried. All their hopes and aspirations for three and a half years had suddenly vanished. The ambitions to hold key offices in His future kingdom (*Matthew 20: 20-23; Mark 10: 35-40*) had suddenly collapsed like a house of cards.

Now the disciples are thrown into confusion. The leader, the ministry, the means of livelihood, and the job and personal security were all gone in a hit. The disciples are not just confused but they are discouraged, in despair and directionless. Peter's discouragement was compounded by the apparent uncertainty about the resurrection of Jesus (*Luke 24:12*). In the midst of all these, the natural leader in Peter came to the fore. You can almost hear his mind ticking: *'Well, if the ministry is no more an option; if these three and a half years of success and acclaim were all but a dream; if there is no more future in fishing for men (Matthew 16:18), surely there is a past to which I can return. I was a fisher of cod and catfish before converting to a fisher of man. If being a fisher of man is not working, I will go back to being a fisherman. I must put something on my family's table'*. The other disciples buy the idea en mass. Such was the gravity of Peter's influence on the floor of the Board of Disciples.

Simple and sensible decision, you may think, until you consider the implications. By one hasty decision in a low moment of discouragement, Peter and the others were about to jeopardize their destiny in God forever. These men were about to throw three and a half years of mentoring by the greatest ministry leader of all time down the drain. The disciples were on the brink of forfeiting the opportunity to have their names forever etched on the annals of history. This bunch of ex fishermen and their comrades were on the verge of walking away from a lifetime opportunity of being the pioneers of the New Testament Church. These guys were desperately close to throwing away their destiny in God forever. The idea of going back to fishing had to have been from the devil.

What happened to the promise of sitting with Jesus, judging the twelve tribes of Israel? (*Matthew 19: 28*). What happened to the promise of getting back more brothers, sisters, houses etc in this life and the life to come? (*Matthew 19:29*). Friend, be careful what decision you make in your moment of discouragement. Like the children of Israel, who often threatened to abandon the exodus and return to Egypt, Peter and his pals were about to quit the adventure into the promises of the future and embrace the limitations and bondage of the past.

Peter's idea was not just a proposal for a career move from ministry back to fishing. So much more hung in the balance. How about the very purpose why Jesus came to the earth, which hung entirely on these men at this point in human history? How about the fact that God was depending on these men not only to spread the gospel in Israel after Jesus' ascension, but also to take the good news to the Gentile world? How about the destiny of generations of Christians of all colours, creed and countries who would never have come to salvation except through the message of these disciples?

In fact, there is no New Testament Christian, dead or alive, who would not have been affected by Peter's decision. We all heard the salvation message either directly or indirectly through these disciples or through somebody who heard it from them and passed it down to us through the generations.

All these said, God can never be strapped for options. Even if Peter and his friends completely abandoned the ministry at this stage, God would have come up with another option to spread the gospel. The point however remains that Peter's decision had the potential for dire consequences. But thank God, Jesus came on the scene at the nick of time and saved the disciples from making a shipwreck of the faith. With this backdrop in mind, it is easy to see why Jesus repeated His question to Peter again and again. Jesus needed Peter to see the gravity of the decision he had just made and to understand that returning to fishing was more than a career move but an issue of competing affections. This is the background of the conversation we are about to discuss.

We have not digressed. We are still discussing the importance of repetition in meditation. Rightly so, Jesus was keen to know if Peter loved Him more than fishing. He needed to know what Peter cared more about, fishing for salmon and sardine or fishing for the souls of men! But why did Jesus have to ask the same question three times? After all, Peter's first two answers should have satisfied Jesus. Notice that each question produced a new revelation of instruction. First Jesus said *'feed my lambs'* (*John 21:15*). A lamb is a young sheep that has not yet been weaned from the mother's milk. This instruction was about providing spiritual nourishment (*milk*) to the young believers in the Church that would be birth after the departure of the Master. No wonder Peter later wrote in *1 Peter 2:2* that these young believers should desire the sincere milk of the Word of God. He apparently remembered the Words of the Master.

Secondly, Jesus said *'tend my flock'* (*John 21:16*). This is a deeper dimension of revelation than the first. A flock refers to a group of animals that travel and feed together. You would expect animals of different ages, sizes and temperament in any flock. Therefore, the instruction to Peter was, *"do not just feed the young lamb, I want you to also cater for Christians of all levels of maturity in the Church that will be birth."*

In addition, notice, that this second time, Jesus uses the word 'tend'. To tend to a flock involves a whole lot more than feeding. It includes the provision of guidance, direction, warmth, and protection. In other words, Jesus was saying to Peter, *'I want you to do more than feed the young lambs with milk. I want you to also feed the older sheep but more than that you must also cater for the other needs of the whole flock.'* Feeding is about teaching the congregation but tending includes not just teaching, but also the provision of wholesome pastoral care, prayer, counsel and direction for the affairs of the Church. Peter would have forfeited this revelation and an entire dimension of his office, if Jesus had not asked the second question. By all accounts, the repetition had the desired effect. Peter wrote two books in the New Testament (*1 & 2 Peter*), both entirely dedicated to the subject of pastoral care.

By the third time of asking, Peter was grieved, frustrated, bored, even irritated! I thank God that Jesus was prepared to put up with an irritated disciple, to press on with the greatest revelation He had to unveil. After repeating the instruction to feed the sheep, Jesus launched into what appeared to be a completely unrelated subject and began to tell Peter about his future. I paraphrase His Words: *"you will live to a ripe old age to the point where you will need somebody to support you physically because of your age and frailty."* That meant Peter would not die young. This was a very powerful revelation. In effect, Jesus was saying that *"because you have committed to the task I have assigned you, I am making you a promise that you will live long to accomplish this task"*.

Somebody may say, of what relevance is this? Let me explain. Peter's role as the de facto head of the disciples meant that he would be put in harm's way on several occasions, whilst advancing the course of the gospel. Can you imagine, what boost Jesus' prediction of long life would have given to Peter's confidence at those times when he was imprisoned (*Acts 5:18*), or he was on trial for healing the sick or he was detained to be executed (*Acts 12:3-4*). Who cares if you are in detention, to be executed in the morning, when Jesus has already promised you that you will not die young? No wonder, Peter was so sound asleep on the eve of his aborted execution that the angel of deliverance had to physically arouse him. (*Acts 12: 7*). Think about that for a moment, a guy is on death row on the eve of his execution, and instead of staying awake and fretting, he is so soundly asleep that even an angel had to arouse him. From where did he get such peace and confidence?

True to the Words of Jesus, each of those threats to Peter's life came to nothing. If Jesus had not used the power of repetition but had chosen to stop after Peter's first answer, Peter would have forfeited about two thirds of the message Jesus intended to pass across.

So what is the lesson for you and me? Let us take a few: First, notice that the greatest revelation in this conversation arose out of frustration and irritation, which came from repetition. The reason why you sometimes do not get certain depths of revelation from meditation is that you are not interrogating the scripture long enough. You are not churning over the scripture repeatedly enough. After all, meditation is like question and answer. You are asking questions of the scripture and expecting answers in return.

Too many of us stop the meditation process at the point of boredom and frustration. But boredom is not meant to stop the process, instead it is meant to introduce you to another dimension of revelation. Boredom is not meant to be a barrier but a bridge. Boredom should not be an obstacle but a stepping-stone. When your meditation time hits a block because of boredom, rest assured that pushing past that threshold will open up an unexpected surge of revelation. Peter would have forfeited a great dimension of revelation if Jesus had not pushed past the threshold of boredom and frustration.

Here is a second lesson: Based on the revelation from Jesus,

Peter was able to stay calm under pressure in a number of threatening situations many years after, because Jesus pressed past the threshold of boredom. What if Jesus had given in to the pressure and Peter did not get the revelation that he would have long life? Well, I believe that Peter would still have lived long but he would have had to endure needless uncertainty about the outcome of these crisis situations. Do you know that you and I have had to endure needless uncertainty about certain unpleasant situations that we encountered because earlier on, we were too bored to get the prediction and assurance from the Word, which would have kept us calm in those situations?

In summary, repetition will birth revelation in your time of meditation and there are some revelations you need to have now, which will save you from needless future worry when you get into trouble.

CHAPTER SUMMARY

Repetition is essential to meditation because it creates emphasis

The boredom that results from repetition is not meant to be an obstacle but a door to a deeper insight into God's Word

The Key to calmness and peace in tomorrow's threatening situations sometimes lies in your meditation today

Chapter 10

Meditation 24/7

I have been exposed to the teaching on the power of meditation for about fifteen years. I became a doer of that Word only about two years ago. A traumatic experience resulted in a serious and consistent attack of the enemy, which did not seem to respond to anything. I decided it was time to '*try*' meditation. I put myself on a staple diet of half an hour of meditation on God's Word every single day. I did it religiously and relentlessly like my life depended on it. And it probably did!

Lo and behold after about two months, I began to see results. I had a sense that my heart had been so empty of the Word of God that it took that much time to fill it with enough Word to tip the balance and begin to make a difference. It felt like the Word had built up in my system past a certain threshold after which results were inevitable. Sure, I was tempted to give up in those two months. Somebody reading this book is in a similar situation. You are on the verge of your breakthrough, but you are also as close to giving up as the pressure mounts on you. You are wondering why you seem to have put in so much and got so little back in return. Let me encourage you not to give up. Rest assured in the Holy Spirit's admonition through the writing of St Paul's to the Galatians Christians.

> [9] And let us not grow weary while doing good, for in due season we shall reap if we do not lose heart.
>
> Galatians 6: 9

The results, which followed my meditation, were both astounding and intriguing. However, to my dismay, after a while, the results seemed to become static and at a point, they even became inconsistent. I was puzzled. But I continued to meditate daily. Eventually, the Holy Spirit revealed the secret of this inconsistency to me. Let me come back to that story later. For now we will look at another aspect of meditation in 3D.

Meditating on Schedule

Broadly speaking, there are two ways you can approach the practice of meditation. The first approach is what I refer to as the scheduled approach. In the scheduled approach, you set apart some time during the day to mutter a portion of scripture to yourself repeatedly. During this time you listen to yourself speak the Word of God over a particular situation in your life. This approach also involves seeing your situation in the light of the scripture that you are meditating. The process engages your mouth, your mind and your spirit. As you repeat the words to yourself and describe the outcome that the Word of God will produce in your life, your vision of the future begins to emerge based on what you are saying. You begin to see yourself holy and not wayward, healed not sick, calm not stressed, free not addicted.

The key feature of this approach is that it is deliberate and it happens during a spell of daily-protected time. It does not matter if the protected time differs from day to day. The fact is that a certain amount of time is set apart for the sole purpose of daily meditation. This is the more common approach to meditation, which most Christians embrace. That is, those who meditate at all! In my case, the discipline was driven by a personal target to meditate on the Word of God for an unbroken spell of thirty minutes daily.

Meditating on Demand

⁹⁷ Oh, how I love Your law! It is my meditation all the day.

Psalm 119:97

A second approach to meditation is the ad hoc or spontaneous approach. Unlike the scheduled approach, which is driven by a target to achieve a certain amount of continuous meditation time in the course of any one day, the spontaneous approach simply aims to counter every single negative thought during the course of the day, by muttering a relevant portion of the Word of God. Meditation on demand is much more demanding because it involves a constant monitoring of the thought processes of the mind. To succeed in this form of meditation, you must set a guard over your mind to interrogate every single thought suggestion and to intercept any non-compliant thought.

Countering Toxic Meditation

Spontaneous meditation is important because, meditation is simply training the mind's response to a particular stimulus. The best way to train is to respond to stimuli when it happens and every time it occurs. A good example is a toddler's potty training. The best time to teach the child to use the toilet is immediately after she relieves herself in the living room. That way, the child establishes the connection between the wrong action and the remedy and soon makes a habit of the remedial measure.

However, the lesson must be consistent and without default, as inconsistency sends a confused message that the offending behaviour is sometimes acceptable, that is, it is sometimes acceptable to soil the living room. At the very least, inconsistency confuses the child into wondering what the standard is. Why is it acceptable to soil the living room at one time and not at others? The human spirit, mind and body can be trained and renewed by the same process through which the child is potty trained.

Let us say you are dealing with a financial situation and there is an outstanding bill, which must be paid by a certain deadline. You have prayed for God to meet this need; you have also set apart sometime every morning to meditate and confess that God meets your needs according to His riches in glory by Christ Jesus (*Philippians 4:19*). After several days, you can even see yourself living in the reality of your needs being met, at least during your times of scheduled meditation.

The only trouble is that just about the only time you can really see your bill being paid is during your scheduled meditation. At every other time in the day, your mind is flooded with thoughts of *'you are not going to get this money by the time you need it; who is going to give you that kind of money anyway; you are going to end up with a red bill; your credit rating is going to suffer for this; there is just no way that you are going to get that bill paid; the bailiff is going to come after you '*. These thoughts replay in your head almost non-stop throughout the day and sometimes even keep you awake at night.

This is where spontaneous meditation comes in. Every time one of those thoughts pops up, you mutter, '*my God supplies all my needs according to His riches in Glory by Christ Jesus.*' It means that throughout the day, you find your self saying under your breath, each time one of those thoughts shows up, '*I refuse to be afraid, my money is on the way and it will arrive before the bill is due, I am not anxious for anything, I have made my request known to God and His peace keeps my heart and mind (Philippians 4:6); I don't need to know where the money is going to come from, the cattle on a thousand hills belong to my Father (Psalm 50:10). I am not going to get a red bill and I will not end up with a poor credit rating because every hand writing of ordinance that was written against me is wiped out*' (*Colossians 2:14*). This is how to meditate spontaneously.

Let me warn you, it is hard work! I was once dealing with a situation and was maintaining a daily time of scheduled meditation. When I became aware of the opposing thoughts that played in my head all day, I resorted to spontaneous meditation to back up my scheduled meditation. In the course of one day, I counted fifty to sixty attacks on my mind, which required me to mutter a scripture response... tough, right? Not when you think about the benefit of bombarding your mind and spirit, with the Word and with that sort of intensity.

Let me use these analogies to illustrate the point further. In 1992, during the first Gulf War, US led Allied forces attacked Iraq in order to enforce a United Nations resolution and evict Iraq from the unlawful occupation of neighbouring Kuwait. Iraq retaliated by firing SCUD missiles into civilian populations in Israel. For a short time, the Iraqi attacks were effective until Patriot missile systems were deployed to strategic locations in Israel to intercept every SCUD missile fired at the nation.

The Patriot missile defence system was very intelligent. The moment a SCUD missile was fired from Iraq, the Patriot defence system automatically recognised the intended location of the missile and its trajectory. Patriot responded by firing a missile to intercept, neutralise and destroy the SCUD missile whilst it was still airborne in the Israeli airspace. This way, the Israeli civilian population was protected from the devastation that would have resulted from the SCUD missile attack. The system avoided a significant amount of potential loss of life and property and rendered the enemy weapon ineffective.

Spontaneous meditation is your Patriot missile. It must be deployed every single time the enemy fires a contrary thought missile. It must be deployed whilst the thought missile is still in the airspace of the mind. It must be deployed before the enemy missile has the chance to hit its target and wreck untold havoc. It must be deployed with 'zero tolerance' because just one effective enemy thought on target is enough to cause serious damage to life and property.

My boss owns a house in a region of Germany where it snows heavily, sometimes for a number of days non-stop. I once asked him how he kept himself from being snowed-in during such snowstorms. The secret is 'you must not let it mount up', he said. 'You have to go out with a shovel several times a day to clear your door way and your driveway'. If you leave it for an entire day, by the time you get round it, you would have such a mount of snow that you would not know where to start. That is if you make it out of the door in the first place. And by the way, shovelling snow is quite exerting!'

Spontaneous meditation is like shovelling snow in a snowstorm. You must not let the contrary thoughts settle. The best time to quell a contrary thought is at the onset. Otherwise, your mind will be blocked in with a mount of contrary thoughts and you will lose your freedom of movement. This is what the Bible refers to as a stronghold (*2 Corinthians 10:4*). It is characterised by a feeling of bondage in your mind to the point that there seems to be no way of escape. Whether it is an addiction to nicotine, a bondage to pornography, a compulsive eating habit or an oppressive fear of the dark, the same principle applies.

Strongholds are overwhelming. They plague the victim with a sense of being snowed under and snowed in. Like the intense snowfall in the storm, the victim feels like contrary thoughts are coming so thick and fast that there is no chance of countering them. That is a lie of the enemy! By spontaneously meditating the Word of God, you can overcome any stronghold, conquer any bad habit, beat any addiction and triumph over any obsession.

No wonder, the Holy Spirit tells the Corinthians through the writing of the Apostle Paul, that the key to spiritual victory is to deal with EVERY contrary thought.

> *⁴ For the weapons of our warfare are not carnal but mighty in God for pulling down strongholds,*
> *⁵ Casting down imaginations, and EVERY high thing that exalteth itself against the knowledge of God, and bringing into captivity EVERY thought to the obedience of Christ;*
>
> *2 Corinthians 10:4-5 (KJV)*

This scripture is talking about spontaneous meditation. Notice the choice of words, *'every high thing…every thought'*. Dealing with a few of those thoughts is not enough. Countering many of them will not do the trick. Even pulling down most of those opposing thoughts is not good enough. The only full proof remedy for victory is 'zero tolerance' to contrary thoughts. EVERY single one of those thoughts must be dealt with. Regardless of how often in the day they pop up, whether six times or sixty times, the response must be the same, to pull them down by the Word of God.

Let us return to my story about that time when my results from meditation levelled out and reached a stable state. The Holy Spirit showed this secret to me about the situation. The reality is that however much time you spend on scheduled meditation, you will only make limited progress until you equally engage in spontaneous meditation. If you let those contrary thoughts run riot in your head all day and the only time you ever try to counter them is during your scheduled meditation, you will not be successful. The key to meditation is not only to consciously take designated time during the day for scheduled meditation but to set a rule that every single negative thought that comes into your mind will be neutralised by speaking out the Word of God. This is what it means to meditate day and night (Joshua 1:8). That way you communicate to your spirit, soul and body that certain thought patterns are unacceptable and you establish a thinking pattern that is based on the Word of God.

Before concluding this chapter, let us consider how to develop a healthy thinking pattern. Broadly speaking, the content of your meditation can be positive or negative. One of these is helpful and the other is hurtful. One is nourishing to the human spirit but the other is toxic. The content of your meditation takes on new importance when you consider that ultimately, success and failure are both by-products of meditation (Joshua 1:8).

According to *Joshua 1:8*, the secret of success and failure is simple. It is in the combination of what you say, what you think, what you do and what you become. When the raw material of this process is positive, the outcome is success. When the ingredient is negative, the outcome is failure. This is the reason why God did not leave the choice of what to think down to our whims and caprices.

> [8] *Finally, brethren, whatever things are true, whatever things are noble, whatever things are just, whatever things are pure, whatever things are lovely, whatever things are of good report, if there is any virtue and if there is anything praiseworthy—meditate on these things.*
>
> *Philippians 4:8*

This is the acid test for any thought that requests entry to your mind. There ought to be a sentry on guard at the door of your mind, interrogating every thought caller and asking, *'are you true or false, are you real or phoney; what is your stand on fairness and equity, how about your hygiene, are you pure or filthy? Are you noble or dishonourable, tell me about your report, is it good or bad? When I finish entertaining you, am I going to be lifted or deflated? What is your intention, to make me glad or depressed? Are you coming to appeal to a moral weakness or strengthen a virtue, is it your intention to discredit another individual or to draw my attention to somebody's success story?'*

If you would learn to set a watch over your mind in this manner, you are about to wave a permanent good bye to your days of defeat. Depression is about to permanently forget your home address. Guilty conscience, insecurity, and a sense of inadequacy are about to permanently break their diplomatic ties with you. Your friendship with inferiority complex, feelings of insignificance and poor self-esteem is about to suffer irreparable damage. Your addiction to nicotine is about to suffer a fatal blow and you are about to discover irreconcilable differences between you and your old unhealthy mindset! We will study more on the effects of meditation on the mind in the next chapter.

CHAPTER SUMMARY

There are two types of meditation: scheduled (meditation by timetable) and spontaneous meditation (meditation on demand). You must learn to practice both

Consistent meditation conditions your mind and body to respond appropriately to particular stimuli

To be successful in life, you must take responsibility for managing every thought that crosses your mind and be selective on which ones you allow to linger

Chapter 11

Meditation and the Mind

[4] *(For the weapons of our warfare are not carnal, but mighty through God to the pulling down of strong holds ;)*
[5] *Casting down imaginations, and every high thing that exalteth itself against the knowledge of God, and bringing into captivity every thought to the obedience of Christ;*

2 Corinthians 10:4-5

*N*otice that the scripture above talks about strongholds; negative strongholds in this case. Sadly, the term *'stronghold'* has been misunderstood to always connote a negative meaning. However, stronghold is a combination of two words: *'strong'* and *'hold'*. So in its basic form, a stronghold simply means to exert a hold of a strong nature on a person, or a location. In other words, a stronghold exercises control over that person or location. Therefore, strongholds are not invariably negative by nature. They can be positive or negative depending on the nature of the party exercising the hold. For example, several passages in the book of Psalms refer to God as our stronghold (*Psalms 9:9; 18: 2; 27:1*). Since God is a positive influence, His stronghold can only be positive. We saw earlier that God and His Word are one. If God is a stronghold then His Word is also a stronghold.

Also notice the words used in relation to strongholds in *2 Corinthians 10*: imaginations, knowledge, thoughts. These are words that pertain to the mind. Your imaginations, knowledge and thoughts are all products of your mind. Here, Paul is dealing with negative strongholds which must be dismantled in the mind. Therefore, in this context, a stronghold is a compulsive thinking pattern. It is a pattern of thinking that has such a hold on the mind that the mind almost always gives in to it instinctively.

It is impossible to practice Bible meditation without thinking about what you are meditating. In other words, just like negative thoughts can build a stronghold in the mind, you can also choose to build a Word stronghold in your mind to the point where your actions and thoughts are automatically controlled by His Word. This is the reason why the Apostle Paul later admonishes the Christians in Philippi and by implication, you and I, to manage our thought life (*Philippians 4:13*). This chapter is dedicated to the dimension of meditation on God's Word and its ability to build a positive stronghold in the mind. The same way that a negative stronghold makes a person to behave in a compulsive negative pattern, a positive stronghold produces the exact opposite effect: addictive positive behaviour.

A man or woman who has a stronghold of fear of bankruptcy and failure in their mind will always respond to a negative news item on the economy in fear and terror; but given the same situation, a man who has a stronghold of faith in God's ability to provide in tough times will respond with courage and an expectation to thrive and succeed even in an hostile economy. It is not about what is happening around you but what is happening within you.

So, how exactly does Bible meditation build a positive stronghold in the mind? Let us study *Hebrews 5: 12-14*:

> ^{12} *For though by this time you ought to be teachers, you need someone to teach you again the first principles of the oracles of God; and you have come to need milk and not solid food.*
> ^{13} *For everyone who partakes only of milk is unskilled in the word of righteousness, for he is a babe.*
> ^{14} *But solid food belongs to those who are of full age, that is, those who by reason of use have their senses exercised to discern both good and evil.*
>
> *Hebrews 5: 12-14*

It is obvious that the writer of Hebrews is referring here to the application of God's Word. He uses words like '*teach*', '*principles*', '*oracles*', '*milk*' (*1 Peter 2:2*) '*solid food*' and '*Word of righteousness*'. This passage also clearly states that through constant use and exercise, it is possible to come to a level where your senses are so developed by the Word of God, that they can instinctively tell the difference between good and evil. This is the level of maturity (*full age*) to which we must all aspire.

In Chapter 8, I stated that meditation must be done in a repetitive manner, quite similar to physical exercise. Meditation in the Word is spiritual exercise. Notice that *verse 14* of this passage says something revealing: '*by reason of use have their senses exercised to discern both good and evil*'. In other words, repeated exercise in the Word of God has a certain effect on the senses. It trains the senses to discern. Your human soul is made up of your emotions, intellect and will. Another word for the intellect is sense. So we can infer that repeated exercise in the Word of God by meditation trains the senses.

The first thing you must know is that, negative or positive, strongholds are not built in a day or two, but usually over a period of years of exercise. In the same way that your muscles and physical fitness are developed gradually through exercise, your senses develop discernment gradually through exposure to the Word of God. Look again at the selection of phrases in *verses 13 and 14 of Hebrews 5*: un-skill (ed), reason of use, exercise (d). All of these words paint a picture of repetition. So this passage refers to the repetitive nature of meditation which we studied in the Chapter 8.

Secondly, strongholds are built one thought at a time. In one sense, a stronghold is a house of thoughts. Once a house is built, it takes a huge effort to pull it down. For example a stronghold of bitterness and self degradation takes a longtime to build, sometimes an entire lifetime. Once it is built, it becomes a towering edifice of negative thought patterns which become the norm in a person's mind.

Your own situation may not be negative emotions; it may be your weight. Let's say, you overeat and many times you have had that second helping before even thinking about it. Here is what is happening: You see that yummy doughnut and your emotions scream: '*I am hungry, I need to eat now*'. Before your intellect had time to consider whether this was a legitimate claim, the jam doughnut was already halfway down your tummy. Your emotion argued so strong that your intellect had no chance of mounting a rationale defence. Before you knew what was happening, your will had kicked in and succumbed to the emotions. Given the same scenario, when you start to meditate on the Word of God about self control and you start repeating scriptures on the subject to your self daily, you will gradually find that the Word is building a stronghold in your mind. When you start saying repeatedly several times a day: '*I am in control of all my appetites, I eat only when, what and how much I want to eat; I am exercising the fruit of the spirit of self control* (*Galatians 5: 23*), you will gradually start noticing changes.

The Word goes to work on your intellect. The next time your emotion screams for doughnut, you will find that your intellect (*senses*) have been strengthened by exercising in the Word. Instead of just caving in, your intellect mounts a strong challenge that says, *No! we are not having that extra doughnut because, we just finished a three course meal, have not exercised for three days and need to lose two stones.* At this point your will kicks in as the umpire that casts the deciding vote. Because of the strength of the argument of your intellect which is influenced by the Word of God, your will rules against the emotions and the jam doughnut.

As you exercise your senses more in this manner by meditating on the Word of God, the Word starts to affect your emotions to the point where its craving for unhealthy food begins to diminish. If you continue, you will get to a point where the emotions completely lose the craving and your whole soul is possessed by the life of the Word of God in that area (*Luke 21:19*). How do you get to this stage? When you start exposing your mind to the influence of God's Word through repetitive, focused, daily meditation, the Word starts to dismantle the towering edifice of self indulgence and indiscipline one thought at a time. The Word of God then begins to challenge your paradigms and the very foundations of your thought life in this area.

After a while, the Word begins to build a positive stronghold. Self indulgence is replaced with self control, excesses with moderation, and incontinence with self discipline. The positive stronghold of the Word of God now begins to automatically repel any attack of old destructive thinking patterns of over indulgence.

You may be unaware that there are millions of invisible strands of hair in your nostrils. The function of these tiny structures is to eject any foreign body that comes in through your nostrils, preventing them from reaching the more sensitive parts of your respiratory system. When a foreign particle lands on one of these strands of hair, it is automatically flicked on to a neighbouring strand closer to the entry to the nose. Each subsequent strand of hair repeats a similar action until a wave action starts in the nostrils, which ends up forcefully ejecting the foreign particle. This is what we describe as sneezing in lay man terms.

Consistent mediation in the Word of God sets up a system in your mind similar to the defence system in your respiratory organs. The word builds up a stronghold that automatically repels and forcefully ejects any negative thoughts at the first hint. You reach a point where your mind is so brainwashed in the Word that it automatically convulses and throws out the offending thought. This is the point where your mind finds any thought contrary to the Word of God repulsive. Now you can say like David: *Your word I have hidden in my heart that I might not sin against you* (*Psalm 119:11*). At this stage, your ability to maintain the desired body weight is not founded in your will power, but in the proclamation of the Word of God that you have the fruit of self control. This is how a dimension of the power of the Word of God is unleashed by meditation. This is meditation in 3D!

CHAPTER SUMMARY

The subject of your meditation will eventually build a stronghold in your mind. A positive stronghold is the key to success and a negative stronghold produces failure

A stronghold is simply an addictive or compulsive thinking pattern which produces a certain response in a particular situation

Consistent meditation in God's Word will build a positive stronghold in your emotions, intellect and will to the point where the right response becomes addictive

Chapter 12

Meditated Success

⁸ This Book of the Law shall not depart from your mouth, but you shall meditate in it day and night, that you may observe to do according to all that is written in it. For then you will make your way prosperous, and then you will have good success.

Joshua 1: 8

*L*et me start this chapter by emphasising a point I made in Chapter 8. *Joshua 1:8* is God's blueprint for success in any life endeavour. Let us summarise what God said:

- The book of the law shall not depart from your mouth-what you SAY

- You shall meditate on it day and night-what you THINK

- You will observe to do what is written in it-what you DO

- Then you will prosper and have 'good' success-what you BECOME

In this chapter, I want to show you in a practical sense, how meditation on the Word of God leads to success in life. However, before considering the benefits of meditation, we ought to define the kind of success that results from its practice.

Good Success, Ordinary Success, Bad Success

Few Bible characters come more successful than Joshua. His very life was a symbolism of success. He single-handedly led Israel into the Promised Land after taking over from Moses. He led a military escapade that saw the conquest of thirty-one kings and the takeover of their territories in just seven years. He competently administered the distribution of the conquered territory to the Israeli tribes (*Joshua 11:12, 16, 18; 12:24*). Joshua was successful, no doubt about that. How did he have such good success? We know that God gave him a recipe for success in *Joshua 1:8*. Since he turned out a success, what is it that we can deduce? He must have followed God's recipe. He obeyed God, meditated His Word, practiced the Word and ended up a signpost of success. In case, you are in any doubt look at *Joshua 11:15*:

> ¹⁵ *As the LORD had commanded Moses his servant, so Moses commanded Joshua, and so Joshua did. He left nothing undone of all that the LORD had commanded Moses.*
>
> *Joshua 11:15*

God was careful to specify to Joshua, the kind of success that comes from meditation: '*good*' success! The inferences are that success is not necessarily good and if there is good success then of necessity there has to be bad success or ordinary success. There is success and there is good success. You have probably heard the analogy about executives climbing the corporate ladder. Ordinary success is climbing the corporate ladder to the top, only to find out that it was resting on the wrong wall all along. Good success, in contrast, does not just get to the top but it climbs the right ladder, leaning on the right wall. Ordinary success is getting to the top of the corporate ladder but paying the price in bad health, a broken marriage and wayward children. Good success, is getting to the top of the corporate ladder intact, with your spouse and children all serving God.

Put on your 3D goggles and see how meditation pans out to success. Here are several simple reasons why meditation leads to good success.

Key To Creativity

The first benefit of meditation is that it is the key to creativity. It is obvious how creativity is associated with success. It does not matter whether you are a homemaker, doctor, plumber or businessperson. If you can somehow increase your creativity, you will undoubtedly increase your level of success.

I am not necessarily referring to an outstanding invention that will make you a global phenomenon. Let us take the simple example of the use of your time. What if you discovered a creative idea that saves an hour on your daily schedule? In one week, you would save seven hours, in just one year you would have saved yourself 365 hours. Do the maths! That is equal to a saving of 48 ½-work days every year. Just to help you put things into perspective, this is about two years worth of holiday allowance for most employees. Think of what you can achieve with this amount of extra time at your disposal.

Think Like God

[8] *For My thoughts are not your thoughts, Nor are your ways My ways,"*
says the LORD.
[9] *For as the heavens are higher than the earth, So are My ways higher*
than your ways, And My thoughts than your thoughts.
[10] *For as the rain comes down, and the snow from heaven, And do not*
return there, But water the earth, And make it bring forth and bud,
That it may give seed to the sower , And bread to the eater,
[11] *So shall My word be that goes forth from My mouth; It shall not*
return to Me void, But it shall accomplish what I please, And it shall
prosper in the thing for which I sent it

Isaiah 55:8-11

There are a number of ways that meditation in God's Word increases your creative capacity. First, the entire process of meditation is an exposure to the Word of God. The Word of God is actually His thought in written form. Therefore, mediation exposes you to the thoughts of God. Meditation is tantamount to exposing yourself to a degree of thought that is far higher than human thought. That in itself already gives you a head start for success, in a world that is full of people who transact at a lower level of intellectual power. Add to that, God's guarantee in *Isaiah 55:11* that it is impossible for that Word, to which meditation exposes you, to fall to the ground without producing result and you are on to a recipe for great success.

There is absolutely nothing more creative than the thought of the God who created the entire heaven and earth. It does not get more creative than the 'brain' behind the universe! What can be more creative than the thought of the only wise God (*1 Timothy 1:17, Jude 25*)? God is so smart that, His foolishness surpasses the wisdom of man and He can confound the wise man with the foolish things of the world (*1 Corinthians 1:25-27*). Now, how can you possibly expose yourself to this dimension of wisdom through meditation and not become creative?

Listen to the first hand testimony of somebody who has 'been there, done that' and got the accolades:

> [99] *I have more understanding than all my teachers, For Your testimonies are my meditation.*
> [100] *I understand more than the ancients, because I keep Your precepts*
>
> *Psalms 119: 99-100*

Surely, a greater understanding than your superiors will give you a head start on the way to success and a better insight than more experienced historical figures is a huge bonus to making it in life. Both of these benefits, according to the Psalmist, come from first meditating on and secondly keeping the precepts of Jehovah.

Since meditation exposes your spirit to God's thoughts and possibilities, it is no wonder that meditation breeds creativity, which in turn breeds success. Meditation allows the thoughts of God to sip into your heart.

See Like God

Besides this, meditation exposes the human spirit to God's light. We dealt with this dimension of the Word of God in Chapter 4. The Psalmist says in *Psalm 36:9* that it is in God's light that we see light. In other words, the light of God's Word gives us insight, direction and illumination. This is the birthplace of creativity. In a different place, the Psalmist says that God's Word provides a lamp for his feet and a light onto his path (*Psalm 119:105*). If you know precisely, what God is thinking about every situation you are dealing with now, you would be one of the most resourceful and creative persons on earth. No problem that arises would ever faze you again because you have access to the thoughts of the God who has a knack for turning every problem into a promotion and a track record of making impossible situations look ordinary.

I am stirred up thinking about God's creative record of accomplishment. Where do you want to start? Let's take the creation of the heavens and earth from a void, shapeless, dark body of water (*Genesis 1:1-25*)? How amazing, that God set the tone by first shedding light on the situation. Some might say well, light just happened to be the first thing He created. I beg to disagree! Do you not see that God was setting precedence here? Creativity begins with light. Science has since caught up with that revelation. We now know that light is crucial to photosynthesis-the process by which plants create their food. Therefore, without light, there would be no photosynthesis. Without photosynthesis, there would be no creativity in the plant kingdom. How amazing that light is so vital to creativity.

Next, we see God's creativity in action with the deliverance of an entire nation from 430 years of slavery (*Exodus 12:40-41*). How about the total alienation of the oppressor in one master stroke, when it seemed that the people of God were stuck between the Red Sea and the advancing Egyptian army (*Exodus 14:26-30*) just to mention a few out of many instances in the Old Testament.

How about watching Jesus in action? The tax bill was due and most people would have spoken to the banker, but not the Son of God. He chooses to demonstrate His sovereignty over nature by withdrawing the funds from an otherwise impossible source...the mouth of a fish (*Matthew 17:24-27*).

Do you remember the woman that was caught in adultery and the mob that was moments away from stoning her to death? I once heard Brother Keith Moore, the Pastor of Faith Life Church in Missouri, relate this account in graphic terms. Just to discredit the Son of God, the mob came to Him asking what should be done to the woman. To say, *'leave her alone'*, would mean disregarding the Law of Moses and to say, *'go ahead and execute her'* would incur the wrath of the common man, who perceived Jesus as more merciful than the religious rulers of His time. *'Make a choice now!'* Choose A and you end up upsetting the religious establishment and risk being perceived as disregarding the Law. How about option B? That would mean a death sentence for a woman, whose last chance of reprieve lay on the Words spoken by the Messiah.

But when life only presents options A and B, the Son of God is able to create and choose an option C that didn't even exist: *'Whoever amongst you who has no sin should go ahead and cast the first stone.'* The mob dispersed quicker than you could say your name! From where did that light of insight come? The creativity of the Son of God had turned a definite death sentence around for a desperate woman, without undermining the integrity of the Messiah (*John 8:3-11*). Can you imagine operating with such wealth of divine light and insight at your disposal 24 hours of the day?

Stamina

The second reason why meditation leads to success is that meditation produces the stamina that you need to put the Word of God into practice. This is exactly what God told Joshua: you will observe to do what is written in the Book only as you put the Words of the Book in your mouth in meditation (*Joshua 1:8*). Only after doing the Words of the Book can you expect to have good success. The progression is so simple. Success comes from practising the Word. The stamina to practise the Word comes from meditating on the Word.

Some Christians worry about not having enough motivation to practise the Word, but this is only because they do not spend enough time meditating the Word. Therefore, they lack the spiritual stamina to put the Word into practice and reap the benefits. The Word of God holds the solution to every problem. If you are dealing with an oppression or addiction; it does not matter whether it is an addition to drugs, cigarette, sex or anger, stop trying to shake it off in your own strength. Just get the Word of God on the matter and dedicate yourself to meditating on it. Devote a fixed amount of time to meditation every single day and watch the affliction disappear in due course. The Word will change your thinking and you will experience tangible success.

Complaining about an inability to practise the Word is like an athlete refusing to eat and then complaining about lacking the stamina to compete in her event. Under normal circumstances, if the athlete exposes herself to the right diet, she does not have to stay up at night hoping that her body produces the stamina required for her event. No! The body naturally converts the food to energy. Similarly, if you expose yourself to the right spiritual diet of Bible meditation, your spirit will automatically produce the spiritual stamina you require to compete and win in the events of life.

The outcome cannot be any different. How can you possibly fail by practising the same principles, which God uses to uphold the entire created order? (*Hebrews 1:3*). Doing the Word of God is simply tantamount to practising God's principles and precepts. How can there be any outcome other than success, if you practise the precepts by which the Most High sustains the created order. Think about that for a moment. How much energy does it take to keep the earth in orbit? How much kilovolts of power does it take to keep the sky suspended above the earth? All that energy comes from the Word of God and all of it is available to you through meditation.

Focussed Thinking

Thirdly, meditation forces you to practise focussed thinking. Most people are not creative because they do not stop long enough to think on the same issue until they get an insight into God's mind on the matter.

There is a lesson to be learnt from what Paul told his young protégé, Timothy:

> [15] *Meditate on these things; give yourself entirely to them, that your progress may be evident to all.*
>
> *1 Timothy 4:15*

Meditation helps you to focus exclusively on the object of your meditation. Paul's admonition was to *'meditate on these things'* and *'give yourself entirely to them'*. Meditation helps you to give yourself entirely to the subject of meditation, with the invariable result of evident progress. Not just evident to you, the practitioner, but also to all. There is progress and there is evident progress. There is progress and there is neck turning, attention grabbing, and respect demanding progress! Meditation induced progress is *'evident to all'*, *'cannot be hidden'* kind of progress! True meditation delivers true progress with compelling evidence. When you meditate long enough on *'by His stripes I was healed'* in (*Isaiah 53:5*), one day your healed body will stand out as the compelling evidence of your progress. Your Christ-like demeanour will one day stand out and testify that it is possible to have victory over temper tantrums, after years of muttering *"I have the fruit of self control in my spirit. I have total control over my emotions"* (*Galatians 5:23*).

Dr. Ed Louis Cole was one of the stalwarts of our faith in the last century and the early part of this century. I once heard him say that the reason why most people are not creative is that they are too busy to stop, focus and reflect. One of the plagues of our time is impulsive and instinctive busyness, which robs one of thinking time and creativity.

I once read about a study conducted on octogenarians. These older members of society were asked: *'what would you have done differently, if you could wind back time and relive your life again?'* Nearly all these men and women said that if they had a second lease of life, they would reapportion the allocation of their time between doing and thinking. Almost without exception, the octogenarians said with the benefit of hindsight, they would spend more time thinking, reflecting and appraising and proportionately less time acting, than they did in the last eighty or ninety years.

You cannot meditate without being quiet long enough to think and thinking is key to creativity. Proper meditation forces you to stop, focus and reflect and these actions introduce you to a stream of creativity that you never thought existed. True meditation compels you to slow down and reflect; acts which in themselves trigger waves of creativity.

The book you are holding in your hand is a product of several months of daily meditation in the Word. I knew I had a mandate to write but I lacked a message. A mandate without a message is the recipe for mark time. A message without a mandate is the recipe for a mess. A mandate with a message is the recipe for a miracle messenger. I kept thinking, *"I know I am suppose to be a writer, but what am I suppose to write?"* After months of daily meditation and dozens of cards filled with personal insight, it suddenly dawned on me that there was a theme that ran through this apparently disjointed collection of divine insight: the multidimensional nature of the Word of God. *'God's Word in 3D'* is simply a collection of the insights recorded on those meditation cards and a testimony to the creative power of Bible meditation.

Compounded Insight

The fourth benefit of meditation is that it gives you further insight into scriptures. This principle is so vividly demonstrated in the following passage:

> *15 He said to them, "But who do you say that I am?"*
> *16 Simon Peter answered and said, "You are the Christ, the Son of the living God."*
> *17 Jesus answered and said to him, "Blessed are you, Simon Bar-Jonah, for flesh and blood has not revealed this to you, but My Father who is in heaven.*
> *18 And I also say to you that you are Peter, and on this rock I will build My church, and the gates of Hades shall not prevail against it.*
> *19 And I will give you the keys of the kingdom of heaven, and whatever you bind on earth will be bound in heaven, and whatever you loose on earth will be loosed in heaven."*
> *20 Then He commanded His disciples that they should tell no one that He was Jesus the Christ.*
> *21 From that time Jesus began to show to His disciples that He must go to Jerusalem, and suffer many things from the elders and chief priests and scribes, and be killed, and be raised the third day.*
>
> *Matthew 16:15-21*

Your degree of revelation determines your access to further levels of scripture insight. Jesus said nothing about His imminent crucifixion and the events of Jerusalem (*verse 21*) until Peter had caught a revelation of who He was (*verse 16*). Similarly, the Son of God didn't talk about building His Church (*verse 18*), an event which would happen in the distant future, until Peter got insight into His identity. Notice the dual principle here. Peter's revelation into the immediate present, that is, Jesus' identity (*verse 16*), gave him access into a revelation of the immediate future of Jesus' death, crucifixion and resurrection (*verse 21*). Similarly, Peter's insight into the immediate present was the launch pad into a revelation of the long term or distant future of the New Testament Church (*verses 18-19*). In God's school of insight, your last revelation is the key to your next one.

I have experienced this personally. Often, I get new light on a scripture through meditation more than I would from just reading. I have sometimes learnt more from six months of meditation than I did from many years of just reading the Bible. At times, I get a shaft of revelation right in the middle of my meditation. Sometimes the insight is so torrential that, I have to interrupt my meditation to scribble down a particular idea, before it is overtaken by the next wave of revelation. At times, the speed of the revelation is so fast that my hands can hardly keep up with my spirit and mind.

Spiritual Exercise

The Spirit of God lives in your human spirit (*1 Corinthians 6:19-20*), therefore anything that enhances your spirit enhances your ability to tap into the limitless resources of wisdom that is in your spirit. Meditation nourishes the spirit of man as bread nourishes the body of man (*Matthew 4:4*). The art of meditation also exercises your spirit, making you more sensitive to God's Spirit within. This is why habitual meditation in the Word of God will make you aware of things outside of natural human knowledge and you will not even know how or be able to explain. Imagine what wealth of creativity is available to a man or woman who has access to supernaturally revealed information.

Let me recount an experience that illustrates this point. I was once meditating on *1 John 5:4 For whatever is born of God overcomes the world. And this is the victory that has overcome the world – our faith.* Without any notice, the word 'pedigree' started to float around in my heart. I did not even know the meaning of the word at the time, so I paused and pulled out my dictionary. I discovered that the word means *'pure bred'*, *'full blooded'*, *'rare breed'*. The revelation could not have been more precise: whatever is born of God is *'pure bred of God'*, *'full blooded God'*, *'rare breed of God'*. Now that paints a picture, does it not? Imagine what that discovery did for my understanding of that scripture.

The fifth benefit of meditation is that it edifies your spirit and helps you to exploit the wealth of creativity in the Holy Spirit who lives in your own spirit.

CHAPTER SUMMARY

Success is not invariably good. Good success comes from meditating on the Word of God

Meditation exposes you to the thoughts of the wisest being in existence, God

Meditation produces creativity, stamina, focussed thinking, compounded insight and spiritual nourishment

Chapter 13

Waiting Until the Word Harvest

²² While the earth remains, seedtime and harvest, cold and heat, winter and summer, and day and night shall not cease.

Genesis 8:22

¹⁹ When anyone hears the word of the kingdom, and does not understand it, then the wicked one comes and snatches away what was sown in his heart. This is he who received seed by the wayside.
²⁰ But he who received the seed on stony places, this is he who hears the word and immediately receives it with joy;
²¹ yet he has no root in himself, but endures only for a while. For when tribulation or persecution arises because of the word, immediately he stumbles.
²² Now he who received seed among the thorns is he who hears the word, and the cares of this world and the deceitfulness of riches choke the word, and he becomes unfruitful.
²³ But he who received seed on the good ground is he who hears the word and understands it, who indeed bears fruit and produces: some a hundredfold, some sixty, some thirty."

Matthew 13: 19-23

*P*regnancies have gestation periods, insurance policies have maturity dates, degree courses have graduation dates, crops have a harvest season and the Word of God has a due season. If the Word of God will ever come through and produce results for you, you must settle it in your heart that there will often be a waiting period between the time you apply the Word and the time you see desired results. The Word of God is not designed to work like magic. It is not a charm or an amulet. As I conclude this book, let us focus on this final dimension of the operation of the Word of God.

The universal law on which absolutely everything in the kingdom of God operates, without exception, is the Law of Seedtime and Harvest (*Genesis 8:22*). How does the operation of this law look in 3D? Here are some thoughts on the operation of this law as it affects the waiting period and the date of harvest.

1. The Waiting Period is Unavoidable

The reason you are waiting for your freedom over that obsession to materialise is not because God hates you or because you are a special case. No! Everyone who has ever produced a faith result with the Word of God went through a waiting or transition period like you.

Jesus taught in *Matthew 13:19* that the transition will begin from the period of guarding the Word that you hear jealously to make sure you understand it before it is stolen by the enemy. Then, you will go through the season of developing conviction in the Word and resisting all the persecution and offence that come against you on account of it. Next, you have to deal with the cares of the world, which try to snuff the life out of the Word in you. All these seasons add up to the waiting time. Eventually comes, the maturity date and the harvest time when, the Word produces the result for which you have prayed and waited. So dig in your heels, hold tight to the Word of God and do not let go of your confession of faith (*Hebrews 10:23*).

2. The Waiting Period is a Season for Internal Growth

²⁶And He said, "The kingdom of God is as if a man should scatter seed on the ground,
²⁷ and should sleep by night and rise by day, and the seed should sprout and grow, he himself does not know how.
²⁸ For the earth yields crops by itself: first the blade, then the head, after that the full grain in the head.
²⁹ But when the grain ripens, immediately he puts in the sickle, because the harvest has come."

Mark 4: 26-29

The period of waiting to produce result with the Word of God is similar to a stage in the construction of a building.

The waiting stage is when the construction site is all boarded up and there is no evidence of anything worthwhile except for the construction activity, which at this stage is not producing any obvious result. At this stage, all the work is happening underground. If you could gain access to the construction site, you would see a huge hole in the ground with concrete slabs, metal rods, and grid arrangements. There would be all sort of underground activity, which is key to the longevity of the intended building. Suddenly, out of nowhere, the building springs up and becomes visible and the harvest is around the corner. (*Mark 4: 26-29*).

The waiting period is a painstaking process. During the run up to the harvest, God gives you something to celebrate at every stage. Most of the progress is internal. First is the seed, then the ear, then the corn.

All you can do during the waiting time is to wait, believe and keep up your confession. This is the point when the seed is dying and growing into the ground first. Jesus spoke about this process in *John 12:24*. Except the Word of God that you sow in your heart grows downward to develop a root within you first, it will never produce a visible harvest outside of you.

During the waiting time the only evidence of the impending maturity date is that you planted the seed of the Word in your heart and given the right conditions, based on the universal Law of Harvest (*Genesis 8: 22*) seeds always grow. The only guarantee of harvest at this stage is the integrity of the seed (*the Word of God*) and the condition of the ground (*your heart*).

3. There May Be No Visible Evidence of Progress During the Waiting Period

Your seed is in the ground and no one can see it. There is not much evidence whatsoever that the seed is growing. However, you choose to walk by faith and not by sight (*2 Corinthians 5: 17*). You cannot see the plant, yet you cannot dig up the seed because if you do, you will interrupt growth and never see the harvest. I am reminded of an experience I had a number of years ago.

As I write, there are two apple shrubs in my back garden. Both of these plants tell a story. Within the next year or two, I will be picking fresh apples from these plants. The plants were gifts from my nature-loving dad a number of years ago. The first one came with the instructions: *'dig the ground, put some compost in, put the apple seedling in, cover the hole with soil and water regularly.'* I followed the instructions as best as I could.

Alas, a few weeks after the transplant, the seedling had lost all its leaves. I concluded that it was dead and it was time to uproot it. The challenge was how do I break the bad news to dad during his weekly enquiry about the welfare of the apple plant? It took all the restrain in me, and my huge respect for my dad, to leave the twig in the soil, knowing that it was 'dead'. I wanted to be able to say, I tried my best. Imagine my shock when the *'dead'* twig started to leaf again at the beginning of spring. The apple plant has not looked back ever since. I was desperately close to destroying my own blessing through impatience.

Do not worry if you cannot see any obvious progress despite your confession and meditation. Do not worry if the addiction is boasting that only death can part you. Do not fret if the symptom suggests it has a permanent right of abode in your body. Do not pay attention if your bank balance seems to be heading south. It is only a matter of time before the evidence of your success becomes compelling. Keep at it and do not give up.

4. The Waiting Period Can Be Uncomfortable

The waiting period is the trial period and it is usually uncomfortable. Listen to the admonition of the Holy Spirit through the mouth of the great Apostle Paul:

⁹ Do not be weary in doing good, for in due season, you will reap a harvest but only if you do not faint

(Galatians 6:9, paraphrase)

Make no mistake about it; the waiting period is inconvenient and irritating. The waiting season puts you in a pressure spot. This is when people laugh at you and talk behind you because your progress is not yet obvious.

5. The Waiting Period Requires Self Control

The waiting period is the stage when your faith must be fortified with the dimension of patience. Those who obtain the promise are only those who operate through faith and patience. (*Hebrews 6:12*) The length of the waiting period will vary depending on the nature and size of your desired harvest, the quality of the ground (*your heart*) the volume of the seed sown and the consistency with which you tend your garden to keep out weeds.

In *John 20:22* we read an account of Jesus breathing on His disciples to receive the Holy Spirit, but they did not experience the manifestation of the Baptism of the Holy Spirit until many days later (*Acts 2:4*). Between the breath and the manifestation, they had to wait in Jerusalem until the promise of the Spirit came on them (*Acts 1:4-5 2:4*).

6. The Waiting Period Determines Future Levels of Authority and Responsibility

The waiting period is what a medical student experiences during training. She does not become a doctor on the first day of enrolling in medical school but she is being moulded into one by the day. The six years of training is the qualifying period. This period determines what can be committed into the doctor's hands. The longer the qualifying period the higher the level of authority and responsibility acquired on qualification.

The servants with the two and five talents endured a waiting period of trading with their talents whilst their master was away. On his return both servants were promoted to higher levels of responsibility (*Matthew 25:21-23*).

A basic grade junior doctor has usually just spent six to seven years in training, but a resident doctor has spent an additional four to six years after graduation and a consultant has usually spent two or more years after postgraduate training before attaining this lofty height in the profession. All these grades of doctors: medical student, basic grade, resident doctor and consultant have different levels of responsibility. Certain levels of authority and responsibility in God are only reserved for the patient Christian. Prime Minister was not Joseph's first assignment. He had to qualify through the ranks of the Pit, Potiphar's house, the prison and only then did he become Prime Minister (*Genesis 37-50*). Often, the Joseph in you is not ready for the palace until he has learnt the lessons along those important stops on the way.

Let us conclude this chapter with a testimony. I enjoy reading the gospel accounts of resurrection and the birth of Jesus during those festive seasons of the year. Recently, I read and reread the resurrection account during Easter. I did not get much insight during this period. Usually, I would move on to another aspect of scripture at the end of the festive season. However, this time I felt the need to delve in further as I had no new insight to show for the two or so weeks of Easter. It was a good thing I did. For the next couple of weeks after Easter, I discovered insight after insight. Had I been rigidly tied to the festive season, I would have been robbed of these precious insights. Persistence and perseverance will take you into territory that nothing else can.

CHAPTER SUMMARY

There is usually a waiting time between your application of God's Word and your harvest of results

The waiting period produces internal maturity but the season can be uncomfortable because the results are not visible

You need self control during the waiting period because the outcome determines your future level of responsibility and authority

Epilogue

A personal experience that I had not too long ago is a fitting way to close this book. On February 27, 2009, I walked past a woman on a sunny London street. She was obviously dressed for summer and had no jacket on. The street was full of people wearing sunglasses, shorts and T-shirts; but only a few weeks ago, there was a snowstorm. As I reflected on the sharp contrast a few weeks makes in the weather conditions and the odd February weather, a flash of revelation came to me about a certain dimension of the Word of God.

February is meant to be the second most severe winter month but here we were enjoying freak summer conditions. Did that mean we were having an early spring? Did that mean winter ceased abruptly? Did that mean that we would have sunny weather tomorrow, the week after and the coming month? I think not. The condition on the twenty-seventh did not mean that winter had ended. It only signified that we were in transition. All the strange condition told us was that there was a season called spring and it was not too far away. You are right to ask me what this anecdote has to do with my subject. Here are a few applications:

- God does not change times and seasons abruptly (*Daniel 2:21*) there is usually a transition. A case in point is the deliverance of the children of Israel from Egyptian bondage. God took them through several stages to transition from bondage to freedom: The birth of Moses, Moses' training in Egypt, Moses' deliverance from Egypt, his training in the wilderness, his call, his response, his acquisition of credibility before Pharaoh and before Israel, all took time to accomplish.

- Transition is sometimes marked by an intense experience of the impending season, which may be followed by an intense return to the old season. Transition can therefore be confusing. Moses showed up as the deliverer of Israel in Egypt, hope in sight, and suddenly the conundrum of transition kicked in and the next thing you knew, the Egyptians introduced worse working conditions. They demanded the same daily quota but provided no straws (*Exodus 5:13*)

- Transition can be a roller coaster that swings from the top of the hill to the bottom of the valley all within the same ride

- A glimpse of the new season is evidence that the new season is coming and it is possible to transition out of the old one

- Do not be discouraged by the intense temporary return to the old season. It is exactly that, '*temporary*'. This reminds me of another year when we had a freak snowstorm in April only to see the breaking of spring shortly afterwards

- Do not stop preparing for sunshine just because of the temporary snow storm

For these reasons, after you have mastered the many-sided nature of God's Word (*life, food, medicine, light*) and you have received and responded appropriately to a revealed Word through meditation, you would often still have to endure a challenging transition period. My prayer for you is that you will not be of the company that draw back onto destruction but of those who believe to the saving of your soul! (*Hebrews 10:39*). I see you becoming more like Christ; I see your symptoms disappearing; I see you being discharged from hospital and returning to work. I see your wayward teenager coming back home and being restored to God. I see you walking out of poverty into your wealthy place in God. I see your ministry and reputation restored. Welcome to the reality of the Word of God in 3D!

Who is God's Word in 3D?

This book is not about a text, but a person. Your ability to apply its truth is largely limited by your knowledge of the personality behind the book. Jesus Christ is the Word of God (*John 1:1-2, Revelation 19:13*) and just one encounter with Him will change your life for good and forever; not just one small moment at a time but in one moment of time.

If you have never made Jesus the Lord of your life, I invite you to make that life transforming decision today. If you pray this prayer from your heart, Jesus will come into your heart and make an instant change:

Prayer for Salvation

Heavenly Father, your Word says that if I believe in my heart that you raised Jesus Christ from the dead and confess with my mouth that He is my Lord, I will be saved (*Romans 10:10*). At this moment, I renounce my sinful past and I believe in my heart that you raised Jesus from the dead. I confess with my mouth that He is my Lord. I therefore believe that I am born again. Fill me now with your Holy Spirit and give me the power to become a witness for you. I thank you for saving me.

If you made this decision, I would like to personally congratulate you.

You may contact me by email at: *words_in_3d@yahoo.co.uk*

I look forward to hearing from you.

References

Chapter 2

1 http://www.famousquotesandauthors.com/authors/martin_luther_quotes. html. Accessed 23rd October 2010.

Chapter 7

1 http://wiki.answers.com/Q/Length_of_single_nephron Accessed 7th Dec 2009

Chapter 8

1 The thoughts I share in this chapter and in Chapter 10 were influenced by two prominent bible teachers of this century Rev. Kenneth E. Hagin and Charles Capps.

2 Over The Top. Zig Ziglag. Thomas Nelson Publishers. 2006.